THE MONEY BOOK FOR FREELANCERS, PART-TIMERS, AND THE SELF-EMPLOYED

THE MONEY BOOK FOR FREELANCERS, PART-TIMERS, AND THE SELF-EMPLOYED

THE ONLY PERSONAL FINANCE SYSTEM FOR PEOPLE WITH NOT-SO-REGULAR JOBS

JOSEPH D'AGNESE
& DENISE KIERNAN

This book is intended to provide general information about financial planning for independently employed professionals. Neither the authors nor the publisher is engaged in rendering legal, accounting, or financial services. As each business situation is unique, questions relevant to the practice of law, accounting, or managerial finance and specific to a particular business should be addressed to an appropriate professional for proper evaluation and advice. The authors and publisher disclaim any liability, loss, or risk that is incurred as a consequence of the use and application of any of the contents of this work.

The names and identifying characteristics of some people mentioned in this book have been changed to protect their privacy.

Published in the United States by Three Rivers Press, an imprint of the Crown Publishing Group, a division of Random House, Inc., New York.
www.crownpublishing.com

Three Rivers Press and the Tugboat design are registered trademarks of Random House, Inc.

Library of Congress Cataloging-in-Publication Data
D'Agnese, Joseph.
The money book for freelancers, part-timers, and the self-employed / Joseph D'Agnese & Denise Kiernan.—1st ed.
p. cm.
Includes index.
1. Finance, Personal. 2. Self-employed. I. Kiernan, Denise. II. Title.
HG179.D314 2010
332.024—dc22 2009031596

ISBN 978-0-307-45366-2

Printed in the United States of America

Design by Gretchen Achilles
Illustrations by Andrew Barthelmes

1 3 5 7 9 10 8 6 4 2

First Edition

This book is dedicated to its readers, who, while striving to get their finances in order, paid their hard-earned money for it.

CONTENTS

THE MONEY BOOK FOR FREELANCERS, PART-TIMERS, AND THE SELF-EMPLOYED

INTRODUCTION

HOW WE CAME TO WRITE THIS BOOK

We sat on the edge of the bed in our friend's tiny garage apartment, in tears. We were ashamed, really, of what a mess we'd made of our lives. We had bought the old Victorian house for under $150,000, knowing it needed work. But it was, in theory (and in sneaky real estate advertising–speak), "habitable." The burst pipe and subsequent flooding of our home had certainly not been our fault, per se—nor had the death of our car the same week—but the costs that followed had shed brutal light on the realities of our financial life and (lack of a) plan.

The beginning of the end came on an icy cold night in January as we were headed from New Jersey back to our home in North Carolina in our very old, very used—but totally paid for—Volvo. We made it as far as Dinwiddie, Virginia, when the car died. Big shock: the cost to repair the car would have been more than we had paid for it. So we bade farewell to it in a friendly mechanic's parking lot in nearby Petersburg, loaded our stuff into a rental vehicle, and hit the road, wondering how we would pay for a new car. We had just bought a house, after all.

Our homecoming was a jarring one: before we'd even slipped the key into the lock, we knew there was a serious problem. Through the pane of glass in the kitchen door we could see where the ceiling, weighed down by torrents of water, had collapsed. Stunned, we walked through the soaked insides of our already run-down home, which we had owned for mere months, and surveyed the damage. There was nothing we could do. It was late and it was cold, so we checked into a nearby hotel, not knowing that we would be living there until the insurance money ran out.

No car. Nowhere to live. But the car rental and the hotel fees were just the beginning. Once the home repairs began, our contractor turned up more problems every day. The heating/cooling system was dead. The plumbing shot. The electrical wiring dangerously outdated. And there were long-neglected structural problems that required immediate attention. Our meager but exceptionally hard-earned savings were drying up a lot faster than the soaked, rotting foundation of our house.

So why was it shame that we were feeling? After all, weren't we merely the victims of seriously bad luck? Maybe. But the choices—the financial choices—leading up to the situation in which we'd found ourselves were all on us: the choice to use most of our savings on a down payment, leaving little to none for our future. The choice not to have an emergency fund. The choice to buy a house that needed work. And perhaps most important, the choice to do all of this as freelancers, workers who, more than most, need the kinds of safety nets that we had blithely ignored.

Facing mounting debt and dwindling savings, we could no longer ignore our unrealistic approach to financial stability. Nor could we turn our backs on the life and career we'd chosen. So after a good talk and a good cry, we had another realization: We weren't ready to give up. We wanted to find a way to make things work.

We had to stop whining and start looking for help.

So we transformed ourselves into personal-finance geeks. We read everything we could get our hands on—the books, the Web sites, the blogs—and quickly realized that independent workers get the short end of the personal-finance advice stick. You'd think that someone would reach out to people like us with serious advice. But most personal finance resources are anything *but* personal—they are all geared toward the assumption that the reader is employed in a traditional job. We needed a book that spoke *our* language.

Inspired, we began to construct what was initially a Frankenstein of a financial plan: in the beginning, it may have been ugly, but it was definitely up and walking around. We slowly—but steadily—began repeating the still-true, age-old mantra that was observed religiously by our immigrant grandparents: *Pay yourself first.* Then we came up with our own mantra of sorts: *Feed the monkey.* We began saying this every time we tossed a coin into our office piggy bank, which was shaped like a happy little monkey. The monkey represented something that needed to be fed and cared for or it would become an unruly, hairy little monster and overtake our lives. We had to start small—very, *very* small—but we had started. As the months and years passed, we climbed out of a negative net worth and into a positive one. We kept finessing and refining our approach, and as our situation improved, the system we had developed remained relevant. It grew with us, in other words, and our success gave us the encouragement to keep going.

Our livelihood may not have changed—we still work from home, we still have clients who pay late, and we still have spells when the jobs aren't rolling in as quickly as we'd like—but our lives have. We know where our money is going and why it's going there. We don't scramble like maniacs at tax time, trying to scrounge up enough money to pay dear, spendthrift Uncle Sam. When things get tight, or a check arrives late, we have a plan and a cushion to get us through. And we sleep a whole lot better at night.

This is a book for people like us, and we all know who *we* are.

We make our own hours, keep our own profits, chart our own way. We have things like gigs, contracts, customers, clients, and assignments. We work long hours, and we know we're not alone. In fact, according to the Freelancers Union, an advocacy group for America's independent workforce, freelancers, part-timers, consultants, and the like constitute more than *30 percent* of the nation's workforce. And this number is only expected to rise in the wake of the growing work-friendly telecom culture and, in some cases, the downsizing of the traditional salaried workforce.

People like us have been told over and over again that going into business for oneself—as an independent contractor, freelancer, etc.—is an elusive dream, one that will *necessarily* mean sacrificing financial security. We've been told that working several jobs to make ends meet so that we can pursue our dreams or better ourselves is risky—better to just "get a real job." We've been told that if we find individual health insurance prohibitively expensive, well, it's our own fault for needing it in the first place. Shame on us for not seeking more stable employment with handsome benefits.

But what if that job isn't out there? And what if teaching yoga or starting your own contracting business, Web design firm, or PR shop is a lifelong dream? If you go that route, then who is planning for your retirement? Who covers your expenses when clients flake out and checks are late? Who is setting money aside for your taxes? Who is responsible for your health insurance?

Take a good look in the mirror: you are.

We're actually OK with that, because in the end, aren't all adults ultimately responsible for themselves? A real job tends to cloud this reality. And here's the final, biting irony, tinged with a little I-told-you-so cynicism: why, if traditional jobs are so great, is our economic system so hell-bent on churning out so many more independent workers? The truth is, corporate America has been shucking off employees in record numbers. As a result, we are witnessing the birth of a powerful, if underground, demographic. When times are tough, more and more of us freelancers are born.

We are writers, chefs, software designers, and illustrators. We are bloggers, sound engineers, musicians, and physical therapists. We are dancers, coaches, actors, researchers, farmers, and even the occasional bladesmith. All of us are working toward a dream: doing our own work, on our own time, on our own terms. We have no real boss, no corporate nameplate, no real cubicle to call our own.

Unfortunately, we also have no 401(k)s and no one matching them, no benefits package, no one collecting our taxes until midnight on April 15, at which point the sum seems insurmountable.

And while there is already plenty to do as an independent worker, many give short shrift to the most important aspect of their careers: coming up with a sound, long-term financial plan and sticking to it. Part of the problem is that the legions of independent workers have no true financial model. And that's where this book comes in, providing what we call the Freelance Finance system and a philosophy for relentless saving that we've developed over the years in an effort to keep our life and our careers of choice on track. This book can help independent workers of all stripes hammer out a financial plan that is every bit as rewarding as their careers.

This is a book for anyone with a job that doesn't provide benefits. It's for anyone who is trying to plan for the future on an income that varies from month to month. It's also a book for the hardworking individuals who, by no choice of their own, find themselves juggling temporary jobs to make ends meet, none of which provide the kinds of benefits that most Americans rely upon. These people are responsible for their own retirement plans but often have a hard time funding them from variable paychecks or even comprehending the products available to them as self-employed. When there is a major emergency, they find themselves tapping into or depleting their life savings, setting them up for a vicious cycle of feast or famine. Many of them earn great livings—but with no system to manage uneven cash flow, poor planning can work against them.

If no one has ever handed you a benefits packet, you need this book. If you cover your own health insurance or are one of the more than forty-six million people going without it because it's simply too expensive, you need this book. If you just had your hours cut back or lost your job, or if you want to finally step out on your own and create the career you've always dreamed of, don't put this book down.

USING THIS BOOK

In these pages you will find a simple yet comprehensive system for earning, spending, saving, and surviving as an independent worker. It can be easily adjusted to a variety of self-employed income styles, fitting the needs of almost anyone who lives from client to client, gig to gig—in other words, it's a tool kit you can turn to time and again. How much to save, where to save it, and how to turn erratic cash flow into a winning savings situation for the rest of your life—these are the cornerstones of our approach.

The book is organized into three sections:

- Part I helps you get real about where you're at financially and where you want to go. Spending, earning, debt . . . it's all here.
- In part II, we introduce the basics of the Freelance Finance system. We discuss the key accounts and techniques that will build the foundation for your new financial game plan.
- In part III, we show you how to expand the plan to incorporate your new successes and how you can adjust and grow the plan along with your finances. And we offer some final advice about how to build prosperity.

Within each chapter we've also included

- charts and graphs to help you visualize key concepts;
- interviews with financial experts big and small;
- anecdotes culled from real people just like you who are struggling—and succeeding—to manage their financial lives;
- what to do: tasks to help you assess your situation and implement the system.

Start at the beginning and work your way through. Whether you're just starting to save for the first time, you've fallen off the financial wagon—we all do—or you want a more organized approach to managing your ample, yet still unpredictable, finances, this approach will work if you commit to it.

You can use it . . .

- to plan for retirement;
- to get out of debt;
- to manage your day-to-day expenses in those months when the pay is scarce and the bills loom large;
- to make sure your financial successes are leveraged to keep you prospering—so that surprise expenses don't erase all your savings;
- as a counterpoint to financial advice given by well-meaning friends and advisers who may not understand the self-employed situation;
- to reevaluate your relationship to money.

And finally—and perhaps most important—use it to remind yourself that you are not alone and that there are plenty of people who make the freelance life work.

Remember—this approach is *scalable.* You don't have to be a starving artist to read it or need it. In fact, as your freelance income increases with greater success, this book will continue to be useful. This system has seen us through good times and bad, big paydays and small. Feeding our monkey became fun. We looked forward to checks not only because of what we could spend but because of what we knew we would save.

As long as you continue to be your own boss, *The Money Book for Freelancers, Part-Timers, and the Self-Employed* will remain the most relevant personal-finance book for you.

JOSEPH D'AGNESE AND DENISE KIERNAN
February 2010

PART I

BEING STRAIGHT WITH YOURSELF

Annual income twenty pounds, annual expenditure nineteen six, result happiness. Annual income twenty pounds, annual expenditure twenty pound ought and six, result misery.

—**CHARLES DICKENS,** in *David Copperfield*

Whether it's a monkey on your back, an albatross around your neck, or some other clingy beast that's getting in the way of your lifestyle, ignoring money problems doesn't make them go away. It's time to take stock of where you are and where you want to be.

CHAPTER 1

CRACKING THE WHIP

Denise remembers leaving her job for life as a full-time freelancer. Assignments had been increasing. The future-project outlook was rosy. Everything had changed. At least, that's what she thought.

"A giddy, mind-numbing joy overtook me when I decided to work on my own. The sense of independence, the excitement, the seemingly unlimited potential! The only thing that could stop me was, well, me. I had just gotten a very small advance for a book. By the way I reacted, you'd have thought I'd been named Bill Gates's sole heir. Visions of the lifestyle I dreamed of beckoned me like a siren song. I did what any shortsighted, overcaffeinated twentysomething would do: I quit my job. Doing this took some guts but also an incredible amount of stupidity.

"At first it was heaven. I stayed warm at home while my roommate headed out into the rain for the morning commute. I didn't have to put on work clothes. I made my own schedule. And more than anything, I was actually being paid—though not too much—to work on a book. I was certain I could line up some more work when I needed to. I thought things would take care of themselves. So I plodded along, made my deadlines. My friends were congratulatory and supportive, and life was good.

"Until it wasn't.

"I did line up those freelance articles, but for some crazy reason the editing schedule at the magazines was not designed to coincide with the dates my bills were due. Go figure. And when it was time for me to start paying for my own health benefits (since I'd said good-bye to those once I quit my job) . . . *ouch.* I looked and looked for decent coverage at a reasonable price. Even the cost of catastrophic health insurance—the 'If your appendix bursts, we'll take it out' plan—was way outside my budget. So I did what a lot of people in that situation would do: I went without.

"Bad went to worse. This check came late, that assignment didn't come through, and soon I was borrowing money. The evil debt monster was creeping up behind me. I was getting work, but the flow of money from day to day was not supporting me in a manner that allowed for even a modest measure of sanity.

"In short, I wasn't prepared. My lack of preparation caused me to risk not only my financial health but also the career I so desperately wanted. Those enticing visions of an idealized lifestyle that had caused me to go down this path were gone. I had to figure out a way to get them back. But I had to do it right."

THE MYTHOS OF THE INDEPENDENT WORKFORCE

Denise let her dream distract her from her financial reality. Are we saying that dreams can't be achieved? Absolutely *not.* Quite the opposite. What we *are* saying is that dreams (and if "dreams" sounds too touchy-feely for you, feel free to substitute "goals," "plans," "ideals" . . .) can only be achieved if they grow out of your reality. In other words, you need to build a bridge from where you are to that dream place where you want to be. Denise ignored the realities of her present situation (limited funding, no financial cushion, no real plan), and it wreaked havoc with the ideals she had in mind for herself (working from home, earning a living from her writing, being financially solvent). Rather than working toward a concrete dream, her poor planning was making her the main character in an oft-perpetuated and usually self-fulfilling myth: that freelancers must all suffer financially.

Ever since Zeus launched his first thunderbolt and Icarus got that nasty sunburn, myths, stereotypes, labels, pigeonholes—whatever you choose to call them—have been created and perpetuated to communicate stories about groups and cultures. Unfortunately, many of the prevailing ideas about freelancers and independent workers are negative. And the myths are so powerful that we can end up believing them ourselves, whether we realize it or not.

"Freelance" is not a word that usually conjures up images of hard work, security, and financial success. People in the arts get a particularly bad rap. "The struggling artist" . . . it's almost as though being prosperous conflicts with the very idea of pursuing what you most dearly desire to do. In fact, the freelance life is often viewed by those in the nine-to-five world as—let's be honest—kinda slack and self-indulgent. Any independent worker knows that this is far from true. But this doesn't stop friends in offices from calling in the middle of the day to ask, innocently, "What are you doing?"

Who, me? Oh, I'm just lying here, stretched out on the old sofa, one finger up my nose, the other hand in a bag of chips, watching a couple of aesthetically challenged midlifers redoing their home and arguing over what a Tuscan kitchen is. . . .

What do you think we're doing? We're working, you nit!

And then there are independent workers who, though they may labor away in offices, are struggling to create a secure financial lifestyle in a larger society that often believes that the only key to security and prosperity is a traditional job.

For a growing number of us, that's either not what we want or simply not an option.

Remember: how the outside world sees you and how you see yourself are two different things. Give in to the "creative people aren't good with money" mind-set, and guess what? You can kiss your sweet financial patootie and any chance of a comfy retirement good-bye. Accept the idea that the self-employed are destined to work like rat dogs with no financial security until their stubby little fingers can't QWERTY anymore, and you can go ahead and start collecting cats now.

Contrary to popular belief, anyone who is supporting herself as a freelance or self-employed *anything* is working. *A lot.* Not only that, but independent workers must toil harder than salaried employees at managing their money, because no one else is doing it for them. While it's frustrating to be misunderstood by those who think you're leading a bonbons-for-breakfast kind of life, what's more important—especially to your money-management health—is how you view yourself. It's time for you to see yourself succeeding and achieving; otherwise, the money that comes into your life will slip away.

WE THE PEOPLE . . . A MANIFESTO FOR THE REST OF US

As you move through your day, take stock of the different people you encounter: secretaries, construction workers, waitstaff, real estate agents, landscapers . . . and remind yourself that they, too, may be working from client to client. They, too, are wondering how to deal with the rising cost of health care. They, too, are struggling to save for retirement without the benefit of a 401(k). Look at them, and feel the solidarity rising up within you.

Look at them and know: you are not alone.

Make no mistake: *the independent worker is the future of the American workforce.* Our numbers are growing, and in tough economic times, they increase a lot—and do so very quickly.

Some people choose to be out on their own. But lots of folks reading this book don't want to be in a work situation where there is no health care, no retirement, no paid vacation. But hey—they are anyway. Nearly 2.6 million people lost their jobs in 2008 alone, and the nation racked up another 3.4 million job losses between January and October of 2009. Many of those workers will never reenter the traditional workforce, instead joining the ranks of independent workers. A design firm lays off employees, and suddenly those ex-staff are competing with you for freelance assignments. A plant closes, and suddenly folks show up asking for shifts at your restaurant. A housing crisis hits, and there are just as many carpenters but a pitiful amount of new construction. What then?

Having your financial house in order brings peace of mind. It also puts you in a better position to survive and thrive, no matter what the economic climate.

After all, anyone who knows how to run a business, generate income, manage money, interact with customers and clients—all on his or her own—is going to be a lot better off and feel more secure than someone who has "job security." In reality, those with job security are subject to the whims of moody bosses and scheming coworkers and are forever dreading that they will one day hear two words: "You're fired." (Or these nine: "I'm sorry, but we have to lay you off.")

Language is powerful stuff. As you read this book, you'll

notice that we often lump all our target readers under the umbrella term "independent worker." Here's why: we want you to start seeing yourself as part of a larger community that is rapidly becoming a political force.

We are the independent workforce. We are prosperous. We are freelancers, permalancers, temps, consultants, contractors, self-employed, self-reliable, self-starters, and we are here to stay.

A LEXICON OF INDEPENDENT WORKERS

People who work for themselves face similar challenges but are often described differently. Here, we attempt to confuse you all the more.

Consultant: Often a once gainfully employed individual who either got fed up and quit or was shown the door by an ungrateful employer. Fleet of foot and nimble minded, consultants have rebranded themselves as saviors to the soulless creatures who gave them the boot. Their revenge? This time, they're charging by the hour.

Day laborer: Workers who typically hire themselves out for a single day for cash pay. The nation would grind to a halt if these overworked and underappreciated workers walked off the job.

Independent contractor, freelancer: Often used interchangeably. Workers who call themselves freelancers are often people in creative fields: designers, bloggers, producers, animators, software developers, etc. They find their own gigs, do their own invoicing, and are responsible for . . . everything. Little-known fact: the term "freelance" originated in medieval times and referred to mercenary knights who were *free* to point their *lance* at anyone.

Part-timer: A person who works less than a full, forty-hour work week—sometimes by choice, so he or she can fulfill other obligations, such as child rearing, schoolwork, or the demands of another job.

Permalancer: A full-time employee who typically works at the same job for an extended period of time—even years—without the usual benefits. On the books, he or she is listed as an "independent contractor" and may even be "laid off" every three months, then rehired for a different "project." This way, the employer can justify not paying for health care or retirement. Some permies prefer their work situations; others are silently praying for the night they meet their boss in a dark alley.

Self-employed: Though the term can apply broadly to everyone here, speakers who use the term envision an individual who runs a small business and may even have employees. The overpriced dry cleaner on your corner qualifies, as do your doctor, lawyer, architect, and sweet aunt Tookie who runs a B and B.

Temp: Here today, gone tomorrow, the temporary worker signs up with an agency that sends him or her on missions of corporate importance. The worker never quite fits in or catches on because work at any one place is all too brief. In the end, the agency carves up the pay like a Thanksgiving turkey and feasts upon the meatiest parts. (Some corporations hire temps directly so they can skip the middlemen and fleece the worker themselves.)

THE INDEPENDENT WORKFORCE

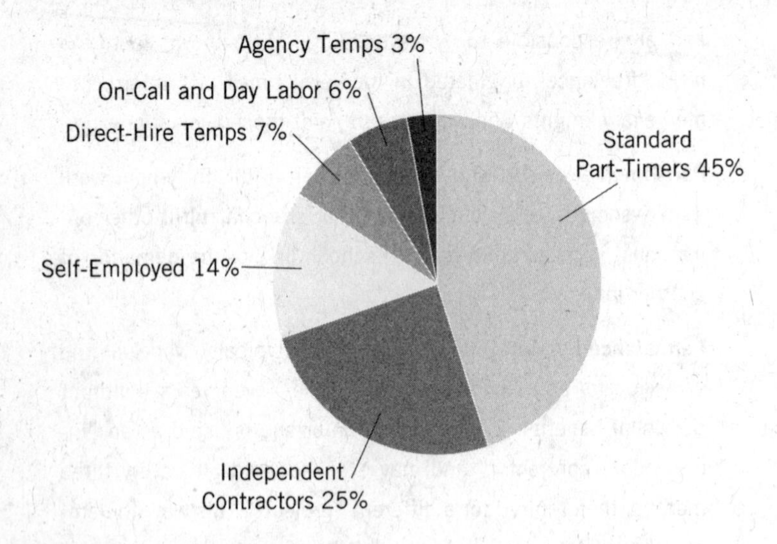

Source: U.S. Government Accountability Office, 2006

THE REAL PROBLEM

The reasons most independent workers have problems with money boil down to two significant things: timing and planning.

By "timing" we mean how frequently you get paid. Full-time employees get paid every week or every two weeks. By contrast, independent workers collect their pay when the project is done, when they book a new client, or when they sell goods or services (once any overhead is paid off, of course). In other words, they have *variable or irregular income.*

By "planning" we mean the complete, systematic organization of one's financial life. For a lot of full-time employees, organization is simply a matter of filling out the forms in their benefits packet. In one fell swoop, they sign up for health care and a 401(k). For the independent worker, things are not so clear-cut. They must do all this for themselves, and often they have no clue where to start. Without *planning*, you cannot have benefits. Without *planning*, you won't have insurance, savings, etc. Good *planning* is essential to your survival as an independent worker.

We can hear you complaining already. *Why make this so complicated? Just teach me about budgeting. All I have to do is make a budget and stick to it.* Well, fine. Budgeting is awfully hard when you don't know exactly what you're going to be making every month. Or you might be thinking to yourself, *Stop the mumbo jumbo. Just show me how I can save more money.* OK, but saving is even harder when things like health care and taxes sneak up on you.

If your income is *variable*, you may have found yourself in some of these situations. Heck, we know we have.

- You spend the first three months of the year working on an important, well-funded project. You send in the invoice, sure that you will be paid in time to pay your April rent. The invoice gets lost, and the check arrives in late May. You're hosed.

- Tax time comes around and—oops—you forgot to pay those quarterly taxes. Now the total is far beyond what you can afford, and the IRS payment goes on the credit card.

- You chose to pay your health care quarterly, rather than monthly, because that means you only have to look at the bill four times a year instead of twelve. Out of sight . . . out of mind. When the statement shows up, you're shocked by an amount that's three times as much as the monthly number for which you've budgeted.

- Work has been pretty steady lately, and you have no reason to think things will dry up, so you decide to splurge on a new computer. Instead of saving for it, you put it on your credit card, intending to pay it off in two months. As luck would have it, your shifts get cut back. Six months later, the computer—along with several happy-hour outings and an occasional rent payment—is still on the card.

None of this sounds new, does it? Well, take heart. Know that your current situation is fixable if you get a handle on *timing* and *planning*.

Understand right now that you're not having these problems because you're not good at what you do, or because there aren't enough jobs, or because you don't have the right company job. You're having them simply because you haven't taken the time to build a financial plan that meshes well with your working style. If you're trying to create financial security as an independent worker, but you are following guidelines that are designed for traditional workers, you're going to get yourself into trouble. It's like practicing to navigate a motocross course, only you're driving a minivan. *You can't really be surprised if you crash.*

WHY IT'S TIME FOR YOU TO GET SERIOUS ABOUT MONEY

The patterns we discussed a second ago are not fun to live with. Yet many independent workers endure them for three major reasons. One, they think there's no way out. Two, they think that breaking out of these patterns requires a compromise of their principles that they are simply unwilling to make.

(This is just the Poor Struggling Freelancer Myth rearing its ugly head again.) Three, they imagine that changing is just too hard. And here they've got a point.

If you think that it's going to be a cakewalk getting your finances in order, snap out of it. All habits are hard to break. Ask anyone who's tried to lose weight, quit smoking, or stop biting his or her nails. The list goes on. But it *can* be done. And it can even be fun. Why? Because every positive change has a positive payoff. Losing unwanted weight results in a newer, slimmer you. Quitting cigarettes immediately improves your health and gives you a shot at a longer life. Getting your financial house in order gives you something everyone on the planet longs for: peace of mind.

Moreover, now is the best time in your life to do this. Why? Because time is absolutely money. The sooner you get your act together, the more money you will actually have in the long run. The younger you are, the better your chances are of digging yourself out of the mess you're in and minting a new, prosperous future.

Here's how it starts. Remember the list of freelancer money crisis scenarios we mentioned? Take a moment right now and think back over the last six months. How often has something similar happened to you? Maybe there was a month where an invoice was lost, resulting in a lost payment. Or you had an emergency that you could not pay for out of pocket that went straight onto your credit card. Perhaps a long-promised job never materialized. You get the picture.

Stop nodding your head. Don't rely on *our* examples. It helps to see what dilemmas spring straight from *your* life. Take a sheet of paper and write down several of the money problems you've been having that immediately spring to mind. (Writing "Need more money" does not count.)

Go ahead. Do it. We'll wait.

Imagine the *Jeopardy!* theme playing here. Let it play as long as you like.

Got it done? OK. Now look at it.

- How many of those problems are *past* financial problems coming back to haunt you—such as unpaid school loans or nagging credit-card debt?
- How many are *present* problems—such as not being able to pay your monthly bills because of tardy clients, lost invoices, or a slowdown in jobs?
- How many are *future* problems—like not being able to sock away enough for your retirement, a down payment on a home or car, travel, or a child's education?

Not long ago we saw a cute little greeting card in the supermarket with this warm, fuzzy inscription:

The past is history,
The future is unknown,
Today is a gift.
(That's why they call it the present.)

While this little bit of stationery wisdom may work wonders on a greeting card, it falls pretty short when it comes to financial planning. Unfortunately, what most independent workers have is a *present* that's burdened by the *past* and threatening their *future.* In other words, they've got so much debt that it's crippling their ability to handle current bills, while the future goes unplanned and unfunded.

Despite the fact that they're running a business—and if no one else is covering their health care, retirement, and tax payments, they are—they forget to *organize* themselves as a business.

TREAT YOURSELF LIKE A GOOD EMPLOYER WOULD TREAT YOU

You may look with scorn upon the employed masses, but you've got to admit: a lot of the hard work of financial organization is done for them. Every week or every two weeks, when they get paid, their generous, caring employers (ha!) siphon off a certain percentage of the employee's paycheck to pay the person's taxes, invest in a retirement fund such as a 401(k), and ensure his or her continued health insurance. In some offices, workers even have life and dental insurance. Once this money is taken out, the employer cuts the worker a check. The worker never touches the portion that went to pay for these three basics.

Now look at the freelancer. She works for a month designing some orthodontist's Web site. The site launches, she invoices five thousand dollars, and she receives a big, fat check for the entire amount. Woo-hoo! No check has ever looked so beautiful, because the client doesn't take a dime out of it. Our elated freelancer deposits the check in her one bank account and promptly begins spending it. One, two, or three months later, she wonders why she never has enough to pay her taxes. She may even occasionally wonder why she doesn't have health insurance or a decent nest egg for retirement. What happened? She was so happy that she didn't have an employer that she forgot that she was her own boss.

Take a look:

	INDEPENDENT WORKER	TRADITIONAL EMPLOYEE
Taxes paid automatically		✓
Health insurance		✓
Paid vacation, sick, or personal days		✓
Retirement plan		✓
Life insurance		✓
Steady, fixed income		✓
Guarantee that you won't get fired	✓	

As an independent worker, it's your job to fill in the check marks on the left-hand side of this chart. It's your responsibility to make sure you are taking care of your basic financial needs, and that doesn't just mean money—it means planning and timing.

If you're going to run your own business, you must treat yourself better than the best of employers would treat his or her employees.

GET ORGANIZED

Federal law compels employers to get their acts together. It practically mandates that they hire accountants, bookkeepers, and payroll clerks to keep track of where their employees' money goes. Meanwhile, Uncle Sam doesn't mandate that independent workers do anything with their money, and as a result, most of us do what comes naturally: spend it.

If you're going to embark on a new financial life, it pays to get your house in order. Organizing your finances will be awfully hard if everything around you—especially your files—looks as though it blew out of the back of a truck flying down the highway.

These days more people are moving toward archiving financial records in digital form, which is wonderful. The more bills we receive and pay online, the less material we'll have on hand to file and store in our work and living spaces, which can help keep things nice and tidy. But some banks, financial institutions, and utilities persist in sending paper statements to our homes. And everyone, not just independent workers, is challenged to organize the seemingly endless piles of stuff until the time that we don't need them anymore.

This book is not about office organization, but we'll go into a little detail here. No matter what system you use or what system you decide to choose, you'll know it's successful if it passes one easy test: once you file something away, you can actually find it again.

Keeping in mind that you need to do what works for you, here are a few pointers from our lair. We've created eight zones to help us manage all of our records:

1. **IN-BOX:** On Joe's desk sits an in-box containing "unreconciled" loose paper receipts from recent transactions and unpaid current bills. This is a *very temporary* holding cell for incoming financial data and mail.

2. **COMPUTER:** Nearly every day, we download recent financial transactions into our financial software program. (We'll mention these programs later and give some suggestions in the appendix.) One of us calls out the transaction, and the receipt—if it exists—is reconciled with the program. It then moves from the in-box to zone 3, the accordion file. Once bills or other statements have

been paid and reconciled with the financial software, they move to zone 4, the file cabinet.

3. **ACCORDION FILE:** Our plastic expanding file measures five inches by ten and a half inches. The expanding file has twelve pockets labeled as follows (your labels will vary depending on your profession):

- Transportation
- Publications
- Meals
- Entertainment
- Office supplies
- Postage
- Trip expenses
- Clothing
- Medical
- Gifts
- House
- Miscellaneous

Don't get hung up on the labels. It's very easy to change them if you find you have missed a category or if you find you never use one of the pockets. Invariably, you will have more categories than you have pockets in the accordion file. You can go nuts and augment with a second file. Don't sweat it. Just make it work. Receipts that have been cleared and that need to be saved for tax purposes will sit in this file until December 31, at which point they will be assessed for the joy of tax season and then moved to zone 5.

4. **FILE CABINET:** This lovely two-drawer cabinet sits next to our desks. Inside, we have numerous manila files in simple alphabetical order. Ostensibly, this cabinet holds only financial files relevant to the current calendar year; in practice, we'd be lying if we told you there wasn't a little overlap. But we are not about rigidity—just commitment to improvement. You don't have to be perfect to get your finances in order. As soon as possible after the calendar year ends, the relevant files should be reviewed for tax purposes, then removed and packed in a box ready for zone 5.

5. **FILE BOXES:** The plastic file holding our receipts eventually becomes quite fat, and come January 1, after we've done all of our tax tallying, all of the receipts are emptied into labeled paper envelopes. These envelopes, along with the pertinent manila folders from the file cabinet, all go into cardboard storage boxes. The detritus of our financial lives sits in our basement until it can be safely shredded: after three years, in the case of deductible receipts and bank statements. We hold on to old tax returns forever. If you don't have a basement, empty a closet.

   Some of our manila files never make it to the basement because their contents need to be kept on hand: receipts and warranties for big-ticket items such as appliances and computers, paper trails for investments that have not yet been sold, etc. These all escape banishment to basement exile.

   As more utility companies, banks, and other creditors have increased their use of digital statements, the number of paper files in our basement has decreased. With each passing tax cycle, we look forward to a smaller and smaller pile of material taking up space next to our boxes of holiday decorations, spare tires, and half-finished craft projects.

6. **SHREDDER:** This sits by Joe's desk, ready to shred all sensitive material.
7. **TRASH BIN:** All hail the greatest decluttering device known to man!
8. **RECYCLING BIN:** Don't waste your shredder's life span destroying paper that isn't sensitive. Ditch it instead in a recycling bin.

Receipts are your friends, and by the end of chapter 2, you will learn to love them. So save your receipts. (Heck, save other people's receipts, if they're stupid enough to toss 'em. Just kidding, Mr. Tax Man. . . .) Receipts not only help keep you covered if you're ever—perish the thought—audited, but they are also the clues to helping you unravel that age-old mystery: *where did all my money go?*

Depending on your work situation, you may need a far more sophisticated paper-management system. At the very least, you may need *two* accordion files, one for personal receipts and one for business receipts. What we've detailed here has served our two-person business well for years.

GET EDUCATED

Beyond getting organized, if you are about to embark on the exciting and sometimes terrifying new adventure that will be jump-starting your financial life, a little knowledge can go a long way. If you have completely ignored—or at least mildly

HOW LONG SHOULD I KEEP RECORDS?

A lot of people believe that they must hold on to financial records for seven years. The details, straight from the IRS, are shown here. Most people fall into category 1 (they owe more money) or category 5 (they expect a credit or refund).

PERIOD OF LIMITATIONS

IF you . . .	**THEN the period is . . .**
1. Owe additional tax and (2), (3), and (4) do not apply to you	3 years
2. Do not report income that you should and it is more than 25% of the gross income shown on your return	6 years
3. File a fraudulent return	No limit
4. Do not file a return	No limit
5. File a claim for credit or refund after you filed your return	Later of 3 years or 2 years after tax was paid
6. File a claim for a loss from worthless securities	7 years

neglected—some of the more important aspects of your money management, you may need a little help. If you bought this book, you're on the right track. But there is a lot more out there to access.

You don't have to be a lifelong subscriber to *Forbes* to get smart about money (although that is certainly a fine publication). There are financial Web sites such as The Motley Fool and blogs such as Get Rich Slowly and The Simple Dollar. Then there's the business section of your newspaper. Making just a little effort to shore up your financial IQ will make revamping your money-managing style all the easier.

We'd suggest that you bookmark a few of the free online resources we mention in the appendix and try them out first. Focus on reading a few personal-finance articles every week. Ignore the (typically bleak) economic news and become comfortable reading advice written for the individual investor.

MORE DISCIPLINE THAN THE AVERAGE NINE-TO-FIVER

Financially savvy freelancers are highly disciplined. True, you may see them out enjoying a long lunch. What you don't see are the weekends and late nights and early mornings and no paid vacations. It's easy to have a retirement account when all you have to do is sign some papers that the administrative assistant plops down on your desk as part of your welcome packet. It takes considerably more discipline to set up your own accounts, dutifully taking money out of every check and remaining vigilant about monitoring not only your finances but financial news and developments, too.

If you have the gumption to bid on jobs, solicit customers and clients, and collect money for services rendered, you already have what it takes to build wealth and security into your life. If you're working two jobs to make ends meet and still managing to support a family, you have more than enough fortitude to corral your finances.

Because what we're talking about in these pages is really self-reliance and empowerment. You may be laboring under years of poor money habits and associations. You can release yourself today. You may be stuck in the Poor Starving Freelancer rut, believing that money does not define you. You're right. But you don't have to let poor management of it hold you back, either. You, your work, your business, and the choices you've made in your career can ultimately get you where you want to go if you play your cards right.

We're talking about discipline, yes, and control. Delicious control over your finances and your future. We say take it. Seize it. Grab it by its horns and wrestle it to the ground until it cries "uncle." *Carpe* your greenbacks, people.

WHAT TO DO

If you haven't already, be sure to do the following:

- Make a list of the financial dilemmas that have held you back. Identify them as past, present, or future problems. Look for recurring themes and patterns. (p. 20)
- Organize your financial records. (p. 26)
- Bookmark on your Web browser some of the financial sites and blogs we've listed in our appendix. (p. 32)

CHAPTER 2

GETTING GREEN AND DROPPING HAMILTONS (OR, WHERE DID ALL MY MONEY GO?)

The blogger J. D. Roth grew up a poor kid who went to college on a full academic scholarship. To keep up with his wealthier classmates, he applied for a department-store credit card and bought a few things. As he recalls on his renowned Web site, Get Rich Slowly (getrichslowly.org), his first purchase was nothing more than clothes, an electric shaver, and a bottle of cologne. But he was hooked. He would stay in debt for the next twenty years.

Even after he graduated from college, he used credit on things like automobile down payments, computers, comic books, stuff that made him feel better about his life. Not that his life was a disaster. Hardly. It's just that, like a lot of people, his career hadn't taken off as well as he'd hoped. He was forever struggling financially. And he had been forced to do something he had sworn he would never do: go to work for his father at the family box factory. By 2004, thirteen years after college, he was in debt to the tune of thirty-five thousand dollars.

J.D. is quite open about the fact that he was once a compulsive spender. Not once during our talk did he blame someone else for his spiraling debt—only his own "lack of discipline." He didn't complain that he didn't make enough money.

Mostly, he says, the old him was flabbergasted at how quickly the debt piled up: *Hey! That money was here a minute ago. Where did it go?* But the truth is, for two decades, he spent *thoughtlessly*, not *consciously*. He spent without giving enough thought to *how* he was spending his money, *why* he was spending it, and *what* the consequences of his actions might be.

Does this mean that every time you dash to the grocery to grab a carton of eggs you first need to run through a ten-step financial plan and have a good sit-down with your subconscious? No. It *does* mean that if you make the effort to get real about your income and spending habits and acknowledge the unique challenges that being an independent worker presents, spending wisely will come more naturally. Completing this step, coming clean about your earning, your spending, and your debt, is the foundation of the larger system presented in part II of this book.

By the way, we don't mean to pick on J.D. (his real name). Today, you may be relieved to know, he is completely debt free and credits his debt with helping him to find his true calling as a nationally known personal-finance blogger. His story inspires the more than sixty-five thousand people who read his blog to learn about getting a handle on their finances.

WEALTH CAN BE TASTY

Think of wealth as a big, juicy BLT. (Or a big, juicy, vegan BLT, if that's your thing.) You're craving it. You've been dreaming of it. Now you know that to build it, you need certain ingredients: the bread, the tomato, and the rest of the goodies, all in the right ratio. Now try building a sandwich that will satisfy your craving for a BLT without having any bacon or tempeh. Or without the tomato. Wouldn't come together now, would it? It's the same with wealth.

You cannot build real wealth without the right ingredients. You must be brutally honest with yourself about three things: your income, your expenses, and your debt. Debt as an ingredient? Yep. While we all strive to be debt free 100 percent of the time, most of us are not. So rather than view debt as something to choke on, take it on. Control it, plan for it (we'll talk more about this in the next chapter), and see dealing with it as part of building your wealth, not preventing it. Supporting your financial life means balancing these three ingredients. Yum!

A NEW LOOK AT EARNING AND SPENDING

Checks and balances. In and out. It's like counting calories—how much are you taking in and how much are you burning? In the case of your money, where is it coming from and where is it going? When you get clear about the answers to these questions, prosperity becomes much easier.

Maybe you don't earn enough. Many independent workers and those who are underemployed don't. Or maybe you'd love to make more money but feel that what you're currently earning should be more than enough to keep you from riding the plastic wave to financial insolvency. In any event, when you need the cash most, you find that it has magically disappeared into some intangible cosmic sinkhole (probably the same one that holds on to the backs of earrings and unpaired socks). No matter what your earning situation, our goal is to show you how to have that cash on hand when you need it—and more saved away. To do this, you need to look more closely at how our way of earning differs from that of the average salaried worker. Take a look.

THE SALARIED EMPLOYEE

- Receives a paycheck that is exactly (or roughly) the same amount every time
- Receives this paycheck on a regular basis
- Receives this paycheck from the same person

What does this mean? Simplified bookkeeping, for starters. Very manageable taxes, usually. Pay stubs are easy to organize because they're all from a single payer. Plus, salaried employees have the not-insignificant advantage of being able to predict their income with a fair amount of certainty. The salaried employee looks in the mirror and says, "I'm a forty-five-thousand-dollar-a-year employee."

This doesn't mean that salaried employees never live beyond their means. In fact, Americans are chronic overspenders. No, what it means is that it's much easier for them to live within their means, should they choose to do so, because they have a solid basis upon which to build their Spending Identity. Your Spending Identity is like a fingerprint. It's uniquely yours. You have a knee-jerk reaction about purchases. You say "I can" or "I can't" afford it based on your own idea about what your limits are. The idea might be skewed or unhealthy, but for the salaried employee, it is at least partially based on predictable earnings.

THE INDEPENDENT WORKER

- Receives paychecks that usually vary in amount
- Receives these paychecks on an irregular basis
- Receives these paychecks from a variety of different sources

Different payers, checks, and billing systems. Payments that come in cash and check, arriving when the mood strikes and the planets are properly aligned. Maybe it's steady for a couple months, or maybe pay is a one-shot deal and you're on to the next client. Remember when we talked about timing and planning in chapter 1? Well, the variability of both the timing and amount of pay makes for some very tricky financial planning. This causes major organization and bookkeeping issues even for the most dedicated. And if your idea of organization is nothing more than a different shoebox for each year, then the consequences of this lifestyle are all the more damaging, to both your fiscal well-being and your state of mind.

A consequence that isn't always that apparent, though, is that as a result of this here-today-gone-tomorrow work life, you may have variable expenditures as well, further complicating things. One month you're working at home, the next two you're temping at an office. Suddenly you're spending on commuting, coffee and lunches out, and work clothes. Any budgeting or planning you did that was based on your at-home work scenario goes right out the old window, and you may find yourself muttering those oh-too-familiar words, "Where did all my money go?"

On top of this, many independent workers have a serious psychological issue that we like to call spending schizophrenia. The lack of predictable pay and varying expenses turns you into a spending schizoid with no fixed Spending Identity. Rather than looking in the mirror and saying, "I make [insert reasonable fixed sum here]," you take a gander at your situation one month and say, "Woo-hoo! I'm rich! I made ten thousand dollars this month!" Then the next month, sitting alone in front of the new computer your home office really needed and staring at your last bowl of cornflakes, you utter, "Oh, *&%!! . . . I'm broke. I made nothing this month."

There is a better way.

So what do you do? Well, if you've listened to us, you've started by getting organized. (If you skipped chapter 1, go back *now.*) Then, before moving on, it's time to take inventory of your financial life—what's coming in and what's going out.

The first step is clarifying the three key ingredients: what you earn, what you spend, and what you owe. You need to find out where you stand. Don't be ashamed—own it, love it. You're already living it.

Our dream for you is that whenever you leave the house you have in your head a reasonable number that is available to you to spend. We can't make the checks arrive on time and we can't magically regulate your income. (If we could, we would have done it for ourselves a looooong time ago.) But we can help you get a clearer idea of what you have and help you manage it better. You may already have a system for tracking these things. That's fantastic. Keep reading anyway in case your technique needs a little jump start.

COLLECTING INCOME: WHAT YOU'RE *REALLY* TAKING IN

How much money do you make?

It seems like a simple question, and one that most people can answer without even a glance at their W-2. But for the independent worker, the answer to this question is often not made clear until sometime in January, when the slew of statements from countless jobs begin to trickle in.

Whether it's a notebook, a software program, your mobile device, or the back of a pizza menu, you should have something to check that gives you a clear idea of what you have earned. Why? When you know how much you earn and commit to making it work for you, you not only *spend* differently, but you *save more.*

Can you know on January 1 how much you will have made by the end of the fiscal year? Who will hire you and how much they will pay you? No. But you can get a hold on past trends and more efficiently track present earnings. Not only will this help you manage your money, but it can also help you decide what adjustments you may need to make to your work life.

YOU NEED TO DO THIS IF

- You are already working independently and need to get organized.
- You are thinking of working independently and need to get organized.
- You earn cash tips or have sporadic income from multiple jobs and have no idea how much you are really making.

STEP 1: BRING OUT THE DEAD

That's right: go to the basement, the storage space, under your bed. . . . Gather up your pay stubs, payment checks, and tax returns from the last three years. (If you haven't been independently employed that long, then just gather the years for which you have. If you've been independently employed for a long time, you may wish to do this for the last five years.) If you don't have three years of financial records that you can get your hands on . . . well . . . that behavior is going to stop *right now.* Three years, people. Three years. Hold on to your financial records for three years. Not only will you be hung out to dry if you're ever audited, but you can't get real about your money without all the facts.

STEP 2: GET GROSS

Figure out how much money you have made—before taxes—for at least the last three years. Be careful. For most of you, it's a simple matter of looking at line 22, labeled "total income," on the standard 1040. Others of you will need to dig deeper because this figure does not precisely reflect how much money you received between January 1 and December 31 of a given year. Double-check your figures against each of the checks you deposited from clients or employers to arrive at a gross income figure. Write down the gross for each of the years you're examining and calculate the average. Are you surprised by this number? Did your income vary wildly, or are you making about the same—give or take a few thousand bucks—each year?

STEP 3: BREAK IT DOWN

Divide the number you found in step 2 by twelve. Circle it. Underline it. This is roughly the amount of money you have for monthly expenses, taxes, and benefits. That's right: it's *not* what you have available for spending alone. (You will explore spending trends more in the next section.) Might you make more this year? Absolutely. You very likely will. But . . . you might make less, too. Best to err on the side of caution.

So we've looked at what you've earned. Now let's look at what you're *earning*.

STEP 4: WHAT YOU CAN COUNT ON

Draw a line beneath the twelve-month estimate you calculated in step 3. Now, if there is any money that you can absolutely, positively, no doubt about it, count on in the remainder of the fiscal year, write this amount down. This is money that might be from a regular client or previously arranged contract deal. It may be money from a part-time job with fixed hours. Indicate whether it will be a monthly sum, a one-shot payment, etc. And write down when you can expect it. Keep this piece of paper in your pay stubs folder. (See step 5.)

STEP 5: STUB IT UP

Save your pay stubs. On the back of each stub, write down where the check was deposited, on what day, and an invoice number if you have one. Be sure to record *every single payment* you get. Keep these in a manila folder in the lovely filing system you created in chapter 1. If you don't use financial software (which you really, really should), be sure to keep a piece of paper in this folder that includes a running tally of all checks deposited. Take any past pay stubs you have on hand from this fiscal year and place them in this folder. Be sure to write down these past payments as well.

STEP 6: GET CLEAR ABOUT GREEN

Cash is ideal for spending and very elusive as a source of income. If you're paid in cash (we promise we won't tell), how are you tracking that income? If you get a lot of cash payments, the temptation to put it all right in your wallet is going to be enormous, and it may take some seriously saintly willpower to break any bad habits you have in this area. It can be done. First, get a cash bag. If you get cash from more than one job, keep a separate bag for each one. This doesn't have to be a canvas banker's bag—although they do have a certain prosperous air about them—the bag can be an envelope or a ziplock. Just get one.

In each bag, place a piece of paper. Every time you come home from work with cash in your pocket, empty it out, count it, and put it in the bag. On that piece of paper, write down the date, the amount deposited, and where it came from. You'll be tempted to simply put the bucks back in your pocket and blow them, but we would argue that you will need to put some of that aside for the future. But more on that in part II.

STEP 7: KEEP A RUNNING TALLY

As you move through the year and into the meat of the financial program presented in part II of this book, keep track of everything that comes in the door. Once a month—which, come on, isn't asking a lot—you're going to do an income review.

- Get the slips of paper from any cash bags you may have (described in step 6 above). From your pay stub folder, get the slips of paper (the ones that show your past earnings average and the tally of your current year's paychecks to date).

- Add up what you've made so far this fiscal year. To that, add any money that you can bank on that hasn't come in yet.

- Now compare that total to your average gross income from the past years. How does it compare? Based on how many months you are into the year, ask yourself, *Am I on track to do as well as or better than in years past?*

This will not only help you spend more wisely but also help you tweak your business approach, if necessary. Also, when cash is low, you will have a better idea of what that momentary situation means in the long run. Instead of immediately saying, *Ah! I'm broke! I need more work!* you will have the benefit of a more complete financial picture. Perspective will rule, rather than panic. *Cash is low, but I'm still on track to meet my goals.* This is also better for your blood pressure. (And if you're paying for your own health insurance, best to keep that in check.)

If you use—or plan to get—a financial software program, it will make this part of the process *much easier*. The cheapest versions cost less than a night on the town, so you really have no excuse. What's better, there are now several Web-based applications (Mint.com and Quicken online among them) that will do the same for free. Even if you don't have Internet access at home, a trip to the public library will allow you to log on and check your accounts once a week. Did we mention it's free? It's less time-consuming than doing everything by hand (although pay stubs and cash tracking have to have a paper trail, no matter what). The software approach is even handier when it comes to spending.

Now you have an idea of what you're making, who's paying it to you, and what you can expect in the coming months. You have begun to create a clearer picture of ingredient number one in your financial BLT: what you earn. Armed with this information about what's coming in the door, you are now ready to move on to examining what is flying out of your accounts—and where it's landing.

TRACKING SPENDING: WHAT'S FLYING OUT OF YOUR POCKET

When you're hurting for money, your mind may obsess on a single, dominating thought: *I need to make more money! How can I get more money?* Thoughts like these—powerful as they are—are tied primarily to *income.* But they ignore an important part of the money equation: what you're spending is at least as important as what you're earning. Unfortunately, most people do a lousy job tracking where their money goes. Independent workers can't afford to slack off here. If you want to be a money-smart freelancer, you've got to figure out exactly where your money is going, down to the freaking penny. These days, this is actually easier and more deliciously satisfying than it sounds. It starts with nailing down two types of spending: fixed and discretionary.

CALCULATING YOUR FIXED COSTS

Every month, you have bills that never change or are roughly the same amount. Your rent is fixed, for example, until the landlord decides to jack it up. Mortgage payments often stay fixed for the life of the loan. Your cable bill rarely changes. Your water, heating/cooling, cable, mobile phone, and electric bills may change a teensy bit seasonally, but even these are roughly the same or are easy to average. These, then, are your fixed costs. You probably have the exact numbers tattooed on your brain; that's how often you've written out the checks. They're the most predictable bills in your life, and they're fairly easy to track or estimate.

Well, that's what you're going to do right now. Get a sheet of paper and write down all your fixed *monthly* costs. We came up with a partial list to jog your memory (see page 47), but your list will no doubt vary from this one. If you rent an office or have expenses each month that are associated with your business, use a second sheet of paper to tally those work-related fixed costs. If you need to, use a month's worth of transactions (from your checkbook, software, or banking account online) to help you along. Be patient. It's easy to forget all the little things you shell out money for. Oh—and if you pay a bill annually, divide by twelve. You're looking for the monthly cost.

When you're finished, tally the total on the bottom line. If you're wincing, take a break. We're not done.

CALCULATING YOUR DISCRETIONARY SPENDING

The second broad category of spending is *discretionary spending*. By "discretionary" we mean "income spent at your discretion." At their peril, people seem to equate this psychologically with phrases such as "beer money." Get this through your head: your discretionary income must fund all the other things in your life not covered in your fixed costs. Your employed pals get a free ride on this: their tax payments and retirement savings are most likely already subtracted from their paychecks.

WHAT DO THESE ITEMS COST ME EACH MONTH?

Cable, Internet $ ____________________

Car payment $ ____________________

Child care, tuition $ ____________________

Health club or gym $ ____________________

Insurance: renter's, home, car, health, life $ ____________________

Monthly subscriptions:
publications, online, Web sites, etc. $ ____________________

Phone: home, mobile $ ____________________

Rent/mortgage $ ____________________

Student loans $ ____________________

Travel or commuting costs $ ____________________

Utilities: water, electric, heating/cooling $ ____________________

What have we forgotten? Add it here.

____________________ $ ____________________

____________________ $ ____________________

____________________ $ ____________________

TOTAL: $ __________

Yours—if you intend to stay out of prison or eat more than cat food in your eighties—must come out of your discretionary income, along with food, entertainment, clothing, and anything else you equate with fun. (Note to sticklers: though we consider taxes and retirement to be *mandatory* costs, we do not consider them "fixed" because the amounts you set aside will vary—sometimes wildly—with your income.)

This can be a massive spending area, and one with a high confusion quotient. You might buy some fancy shoes one month but not the next. If you didn't slavishly log every single transaction, you probably won't remember how you spent your money. Well, not anymore. The confusion ends today. Here's what you'll do.

FIRST STEPS TO TRACKING YOUR SPENDING

STEP 1: GO SHOPPING!

Again, if you don't already have a financial software program loaded on your computer or use one online, look into it. (Again, see the appendix.) While you're at it, register to access your checking or savings account online. Almost all banks provide this service now (usually for free). You will have access to months of your spending transactions.

STEP 2: REPEAT AFTER ME . . .

From this moment forth, resolve to ask for and keep every single receipt from every single transaction you make.

STEP 3: LOG IT

If receipts are not available or you forget to get one, write down what you spent on a sheet of paper carried in your wallet for this very purpose. No amount is too small. Pumping quarters into a parking meter? Write it down. Grabbing a coffee and a paper on the way to a meeting? Write it down. Leave a cash tip at the diner? You get the picture. It all adds up. (And some of it—depending on your career—may be tax deductible. Cha-ching!)

STEP 4: SEEK RECONCILIATION, MY CHILD

As soon as possible after a cash transaction, enter the cash expense in your financial software program. If you used a debit card or credit card for the transaction, download the most recent transactions from the relevant bank account and reconcile the receipts with your bank once a week. If you don't have software, reconcile any card transactions with your bank statement at the end of the month. Don't postpone these steps for too long, or else you'll have a mountain of receipts to wade through and begin to distrust or hate this system.

STEP 5: STASH IT

File the receipts away, in either the accordion folder or the file cabinet we discussed in chapter 1.

If you're already practicing these steps on your own, congratulations. You're probably in better financial shape than you think, provided you have meticulously recorded, downloaded, and reconciled your transactions. Unknowingly, you've been building an invaluable archive that will allow you to better analyze your spending patterns. If you *haven't* been doing this, what the hell are you waiting for? Get on the stick. Now.

A few thoughts:

- These are not terribly earth-shattering steps, but we know a lot of people have an aversion to practicing them on a regular basis. Independent workers cannot afford this. We know people who hate checking their account balances so much that they never cast an eye upon their ATM receipts. They stuff them in the recesses of their wallets or discard them entirely. Get over this stomach-churning resistance. You need to be able to look upon the chaos without fear. Knowledge is power. And control.

- We do not get a dime from any software company or online service. In fact, you *do not* absolutely need financial software to track your expenses—but we strongly advise it. A spreadsheet will also do nicely. For many years Joe tracked all his expenses on tiny scraps of paper he kept in his wallet. Every night when he got home, he'd dutifully transfer the info from the scrap paper to columns in one of those marble-covered notebooks. Yes, this was ridiculously time-consuming and laborious, but he didn't have much of a social life. That said, software allows you to crunch numbers in a way that would be annoying or impossible to perform by hand. Nearly all independent workers we know track their expenses electronically, even the professional (freelance) lifeguard we know who doesn't have e-mail. So you would be well advised to get on the bandwagon as soon as possible. How far can you take the high tech? Many online services and banks allow you to check your bank accounts from your mobile phone.

- You *do not* need to keep all receipts once you have reconciled them in your accounts. (We routinely discard grocery receipts because they are irrelevant to our tax situation. If you are a chef testing recipes on the side for a culinary school, that's different.) Only you and your accountant can accurately determine what receipts you ought to save in the long term. (You'll hear about these indispensable individuals in chapter 7.) If you're just starting this program, you're probably better off holding on to all receipts until you have spoken to an accountant.

WHAT HAVE YOU LEARNED?

What does all this nonsense—tallying income, charting your overhead, and tracking your expenses—actually do for you? It records a history of the very thing you are most likely to forget or ignore: what you make and where it's really going. After examining a few months' data on your earning and spending habits, you'll be able to generate fascinating reports that provide some startling clarity.

Take some time now to do this. Using your accumulated data, can you answer these questions?

YOUR INCOME

- Are you earning roughly the same each month? Each year? Or are your earnings strongly variable?
- If variable, are there big gaps, little gaps, all gaps?
- Just how long are you likely to wait between checks?
- Who are your top five customers or clients this year?
- Were they your largest source of income last year (if data is available)?

- Is there anything predictable about your income this fiscal year?
- Is your income greater than your expenses?

YOUR SPENDING

- What is your single biggest expense every month?
- What are your top five biggest expenses every month?
- Do any of these spending categories come as a surprise? Why or why not?
- Does your spending decline markedly during "gap" periods when your income drops—or do you keep spending away?
- What do you spend each month on dining out?
- On clothing?
- On entertainment?
- If you had to pick one category to rein in spending, which would it be?

EBBING AND FLOWING

We urge you to play with your software from time to time, generating reports to see what you can learn about yourself and your once-mysterious finances. It may be painful to do this if you've never done it before, but once you get over the initial shock, you may find a few surprises lurking in the data. Or not.

Either way, knowing where you stand financially always makes it easier to tackle your problems.

Many independent workers are stunned to realize that they have actually earned *more* in the last three months or year than they thought they had. And yet during that time, they constantly felt like they were broke. What gives? Most likely, people like this don't have an income problem. *They have a cash-flow problem.*

Feast or famine. Ebb and flow. This is the most common dilemma of the independent worker. The long, wintry gaps in income—waiting months to get paid for work you've done diligently, quickly, and on time—mean long periods of scrapping by, living off savings or, more often, credit cards. It helps to stay positive, sending out those invoices, continuing to work hard, all the while reassuring yourself, *Gee, once the money starts flowing, it'll be great.* When money isn't flowing, Denise likes to remind herself that the bigger the ebb is, the larger the wave of cash that will flood her bank account. Envision the wave, of course, as money. It would be nice to figure out a way to hold on to some of that money when it does arrive, to better soften the blow of the next inevitable gap. But how do you do that?

ESTABLISHING YOUR SPENDING IDENTITY

Answering that question is the job of this book. You'll find the main tools you'll need to tackle cash-flow problems in part II. But for now, start by getting a handle on your earning and spending. If you took the time to answer some of the questions on page 52, you're starting to shape your Spending Identity.

Take the time right now to write a Spending Identity Statement. This is a little like a New Year's resolution or a pact you make with yourself—and among other things, it will help you understand "about how much" you can spend on the things you want.

Let's first read the Spending Identity Statement shown on page 55. You can either use this statement exactly as shown here or draft your own. Obviously, you will want to insert your own information in the blanks.

Some things to keep in mind:

- *Go easy on yourself.* Try not to choose more than three categories to monitor during any given period of time.

- *Don't be too rigid.* Notice that Molly did not try to eradicate the entire $583 she estimates she spends each month in excess of her average monthly income. She's trying to get $250 of her spending under control.

- *Use estimates.* Being an independent worker means not knowing exactly what your income is from month to month. That's why you pay "estimated" taxes. If estimation is good enough for the Tax Man, it should be good enough for you. That's why Molly uses words like "about" or "on average" to calculate her figures.

When you're done with your statement, tuck it away in a spot where you are likely to see it from time to time, like the top drawer of your desk. When the time you allotted elapses, take it out and review how well you did and perhaps set some new goals. Ideally, if you monitor your spending weekly, you'll

SPENDING IDENTITY STATEMENT

For Molly Jones

As of 11/30/09, I have earned $43,456.68 in my freelance business.

My monthly fixed expenses are $2,365.

Based on income so far this year, my monthly discretionary income is about $1,585.

On average, I have spent about $583 more each month than my average monthly income to date.

In the next three months, I will weekly monitor how much I spend on

1. shoes
2. eating out
3. hooch

I'd feel really great if I could spend no more than

$100 each month on shoes
$100 each month on eating out
$50 each month on hooch

I will check on my progress on
2/28/10.

Signed, with utter sincerity and not a hint of irony,
Molly Jones 11/30/09

have a good idea where you stand. Later, as you go through the other steps in this book, you will have the opportunity to amend your statement to include saving money for specific goals.

THE POWER OF CHANGE: HOW YOUR SPENDING IDENTITY HELPS YOU SPEND SMARTER

We didn't want to make a big deal about this, but establishing your Spending Identity is really an exercise in behavior change and budgeting. We typed those words really small so you wouldn't freak out when you saw them. There's such a negative connotation surrounding these two concepts that we thought it was better not to announce them when we sprang them on you the first time.

Knowing *about how much* you earn as a freelancer or *about how much* you can spend on various things in your life is powerful. You'll be less likely to spend thoughtlessly, and you'll be less vulnerable to come-ons that try to part you from your cashola. We live in a nation that desperately needs people to spend in order to keep the economy moving. And so you are constantly bombarded by catchphrases such as "The more you spend, the more you save." This is dead wrong. The more you spend, the more you spend. Period.

What is needed to sustain human life hasn't changed too much in the last hundred thousand years. We all need food, shelter, and clothing. Nearly everything beyond those basic needs is not something we *need*; it's something we *want*. Think back twenty years, if you can. Back then, mobile phones, high-speed Internet, and cable TV were either in their infancy or nonexistent. Now, all of us are convinced that spending hundreds a month on these items is not only desirable but absolutely necessary. These costs, which didn't even exist years ago, are a part of the budgets of most American households today.

The machinery of marketing, advertising, and media magically transforms wants into needs.

These days we have mail-in movie rentals, digital TV recordings, and satellite radio, all with costly monthly subscriber fees so you can forever support the fine, upstanding corporate citizens that give so much back to the nation. (Insert sarcastic roll of eyes here.) Some things—ink-jet printers, computer game hardware, MP3 players—hit the market with the carefully constructed illusion that they are cheap. But by virtue of purchasing them, you are hooked on a lifetime of spending in order to keep them novel or functioning. Other devices, such as mobile phones, are really impulse-shopping engines designed to get you to spend ceaselessly on texting, ringtones, and mobile applications.

Don't get us wrong. We're not blaming you. We love this crap, too, but common sense says you can't keep tacking endless costs onto your overhead unless your income is infinitely growing.

You, the freelancer, have to be especially careful. You have more to lose. If you spend money on junk this month, and the client doesn't pay up next month, what will you do? What will go unpaid? You can't rely on a paycheck in two weeks to bail you out. Only you and your cleverly evolving Spending Identity can do that.

If your answer to cash flow problems has been *Whip out the credit card, silly,* it's time to change.

WHAT TO DO

We went over a lot in this chapter. The following will help you make sure that you have a grasp on what's coming in and going out.

- Review at least three years of your past taxes. Compute the average gross income you've earned each year, and what it is on a monthly basis. (p. 41)
- Make a list of payments you have received so far this year and the dates that you received them. (p. 42)
- Start saving and tracking all your income—cash included. Do this on paper for your cash and using financial software (or paper) for checks. (pp. 42–43)
- Commit to reviewing your income each month. (p. 43)
- Calculate your fixed monthly costs. (p. 47)
- Start tracking your spending using a notebook or financial software. (p. 48)
- Draft and sign a Spending Identity Statement. (p. 54)

CHAPTER 3

UNDERSTANDING THE CRUSHING MISERY OF DEBT

Intrigued by our zest, zeal, and occasionally annoying perkiness when it comes to discussing personal finance, our friend Erin, a dance teacher and choreographer, asked if we'd give her a hand. We love a good guinea pig, so we said yes. Her primary concern was her unruly credit-card debt. We ran her through the wringer, asking what she earned from her various jobs as a teacher, as an administrative assistant at an arts festival, and working part-time in a DVD rental shop. And we asked for a list of her credit cards, their balances, and their corresponding interest rates.

Her situation was quite typical for an independent worker juggling jobs to make ends meet. She had six cards total: three were store credit cards and the other three were bank credit cards. Their interest rates ranged from zero to 23.5 percent, and she was paying them off in a completely common but rather ineffective way: sending the minimum to each card every month. And of course, the oh-so-devious and seductive credit-card companies sometimes even generously offered to let her skip a month, which she happily—but alas, not too wisely—did. The balances were not heading in the right direction. And the interest she was paying? Well, it was downright sobering. To top it off, she had no health insurance. Considering the risk of injury that all dancers must contemplate, she was one bad plié away from adding hospital bills to her already escalating financial liability.

We crafted a five-page action plan for Erin based on her income. She thanked us and went on her merry way. We received occasional updates, and there have been a few stumbles (she bought a laptop—on plastic) and some successes (she paid off her car). Saddled with debt and working from performance to performance, this master's degree holder continues to make ends meet teaching dance classes and working part time. She is working hard to pay down what she owes while simultaneously trying to save for a down payment on her first home.

The moral of the story, not surprisingly, is that eradicating debt is hard. But here was someone who sought help regarding her finances—something most of us are loath to do—and who took the time to look over how much she owed and to whom and to create a plan for dealing with it. She took the first step, and her small victories keep coming as she inches closer to being debt free.

SOMETHING FOR EVERYONE

If there is one chapter in this book that speaks—shouts, really—to anyone and everyone, it's probably this one. If there is one topic that resonates with citizens of our fair country, it's debt. Paralyzing, life-shattering, dream-destroying debt.

Somehow debt has become acceptable, considered inevitable even. People may not tell you what they earn, or how much they paid for their house, but it's extremely common to gripe about credit-card debt, holiday debt, student loans, and the like.

Bonding over debt may be twisted or unhealthy, but it's a far-reaching solidarity. Rich or poor, young or old, salaried or freelance, most of us have debt hanging over our heads that we would love to get rid of. Maybe it's a mortgage, a car loan, student loans, hospital bills, or credit cards. Whatever shape your debt takes, if it is not kept under control, it can negatively impact your ability to reach your other financial goals, maintain solvency, and preserve your sanity. It endangers everything from your career to your family's future. Unwanted debt shaves years off your life, first in the form of stress and second because you lose so many years eradicating it.

Enough dark clouds for you? Here are some more.

- The number of credit-card holders in the U.S. is expected to reach 181 million in 2010.
- Americans owe more than $970 billion in credit-card debt.
- About 44 percent of families carry a credit-card balance.
- Americans rack up about $15 billion in penalties each year.

Many Americans routinely spend more than they save. In fact, during the last decade, our savings rate slipped into negative numbers for the first time since the Depression. Financial woes get worse during tough times. When the economy falters, people start to fall behind on all their bills. That's when credit-card companies pounce, levying fees or jacking up interest rates. The result? People fall behind *even more* on their bills.

No doubt about it—the credit-card industry is perverse. Think you know what a deadbeat is? Think again. In the lexicon of the credit-card business, a "deadbeat" is *someone who pays his card off in full every month.* Why? Because the companies don't make a dime off these cardholders.

You can't reason with lenders who think this way. Your smartest option is to get out from under their yoke. Getting out of debt on a regular salary is hard enough. Doing it while living with an unpredictable income is harder. But it can be done. This chapter lays the foundation for the actions you will take in part II to get your debt under control.

IMAGE IS EVERYTHING

Credit is the world's perception of you, specifically your ability to make good on your debts. From the moment you start acquiring debt and extinguishing it, insufferable moles are collecting data about you and assessing how great a financial risk you pose to anyone who would lend you money, rent you an apartment, or do business with you. Your creditworthiness is boiled down to a single number or score. Most businesses use the system conceived by the Fair Isaac Corporation, otherwise known as the FICO score system. (The number ranges from 300 to 850.) The lower the score, the bigger the risk you pose, and so the higher the interest you are likely to pay on your debts. Thus, it makes good financial sense to boost your score and preserve it. Historically, any score under 620 was considered subprime, though lenders have become stricter as we enter the second decade of the twenty-first century. Apparently, it is no longer enough to have a pulse to qualify for, say, a mortgage.

Some tips:

Debt-to-Credit Ratio: Besides paying your bills on time and not applying for tons of credit cards, it's smart to monitor your debt-to-credit ratio. The closer you get to maxing out your total available credit, the higher your ratio climbs. Try not to use more than a third of your available credit, and you'll be fine.

Credit Reports: You are entitled by law to know what the three major credit-reporting agencies—TransUnion, Experian, and Equifax—are telling creditors about you. You can request one free report a year from each company. (Go to annualcreditreport.com.) Request one report from a different company every three months and you'll never pay a dime. You will, however, need to pay if you want to know your FICO score.

Credit Freezes: The best way to prevent identity theft is to request a freeze of your data from all three credit-reporting agencies. Only do this if you are certain you won't be applying for any new credit in the immediate future. Not only will cretinous felons not be able to apply for credit cards in your name, but you won't either. Freezing or unfreezing does cost, but fees are nominal. See financialprivacynow.org.

DEBT AND THE INDEPENDENT WORKER

From the way we joke about employed people, you may get the impression that we think they've got it made. Far from it. Chances are their finances are just as screwed up as an independent worker's. But they have an advantage over freelancers. When they're down to their last shekel, they can kind of hunker down and wait it out. In a week or so, another paycheck will arrive to save the day.

You probably don't have that luxury. When that last shekel's gone, that's it. There's no guaranteed paycheck waiting in the wings. Just a glimmer of hope that the clients you recently billed will pay up. As you wait for them to find their checkbooks, credit cards start to look and smell a lot like cash, kind of the way the Road Runner looked like Thanksgiving-on-legs to a ravenous Wile E. Coyote.

Credit cards always seem like the perfect way out of a financial dilemma. Hand the card over. Let 'em swipe it. *Bam!* Bill eradicated. But is it really? We think not. The "solution" credit cards offer is just a mirage.

In chapter 1, we described debt as a part of your financial *past.* We think it's absolutely fair to think of it this way. If you were to haul out some old credit-card bills from two years ago, you'd undeniably have some sweet memories on those sheets.

You'd also have lots of utter crap. Would you really remember that quick, nasty meal you scarfed down in that airport between flights? The tacky melamine DVD rack you bought for $49.99, only to toss it out when you moved to a new apartment? The round of drinks you bought for those ungrateful friends you don't even see anymore? These are memories you have quite rightly forgotten. They're remnants of the old you. You may think that you have matured, wised up, and moved on. But if you're shelling out today's dollars to pay off something that happened two, five, or ten years ago, you have less money to pay for today's needs and tomorrow's goals. The money that's going to your debt could be going into a health savings account, a retirement account, or a mortgage. Psychologically and financially, you can't move on until you've expunged the past, or at least gotten it under control.

Freelancers are highly susceptible to this trap. Their variable income breeds long income gaps, which in turn can

BORROWING FOR YOUR BUSINESS

Some freelance businesses consist of nothing more than one creative brain, a laptop, and an Internet connection. But others require costly materials, office supplies, or equipment to get off the ground. Before turning to a credit card to fund these needs, consider getting start-up or expansion money the old-fashioned way: in the form of a business loan.

Look for a community development financial institution (CDFI) near you; their specific mission is to lend money to local businesses. You may even find nonprofit economic development organizations that offer small "peer loans" to people like you. See the Association for Enterprise Opportunity (AEO) at microenterpriseworks.org for more information.

Whichever route you take, you'll be expected to submit a formal business plan, a hefty document that describes your plans, goals, and intended route toward achieving them. Writing such a plan won't be as easy as slapping your new equipment on a credit card, but it will force you to think more carefully about how you'll make your business work.

If you do end up using a dedicated credit card for your business, be smart about it. If a client's expense goes on your card, invoice for it immediately. There's no reason you should be subsidizing *their* business. Be sure to anticipate any interest you may accrue while the invoice is outstanding. Yes, you may bill a client for that interest, but you must spell out that you will at the start of your business relationship.

lure them into their credit cards' seedy little lair of financial despair.

DEBT AS PART OF THE EQUATION

As we've mentioned before, you can't build wealth without considering your debt as part of the equation. In chapter 2, we looked at your earnings and your fixed monthly costs. Now it's time to handle the third component: your debt.

In part II, you will take everything from part I and dive headlong into the real meat of the Freelance Finance system. But the system only works if you look at your financial picture as a whole. You can't pick and choose what you want to do, focusing on this part here, skipping that section over there. You have to take it all on: soup to nuts, savings to debt. When you set up your various accounts, the choices you make will depend on a real, honest-to-goodness, I'm-not-hiding-anything account of where your financial life is. *All* of it. This demands total financial transparency. That means that if you have unruly debt lurking in the shadows, you will drag it out into the sunlight, where it's not so scary anymore, and you'll tackle it, bit by bit.

If you are in the clear as far as credit-card debt is concerned, kudos to you! You are a credit to our tribe. If not, you have got to yank those financial skeletons out of the closet and own them. Shout it from the rooftops: "I'm not perfect! I have made some terrible financial transgressions! But I've had enough. It all stops here!" Trust us—this is an important step to safeguarding your dreams.

So what's in your past? Let's take a closer look.

SURVEYING YOUR DEBT

Debt has a way of creeping up on folks. One day, everything is under control. But then there's a slow work month, a few misguided dinners out, the holiday season, and before you can say "zero percent down" you have gone from managing your debt to drowning in it.

It's time to get naked . . . financially speaking, that is.

- First, gather any and all statements you have that pertain to money you owe. Don't leave anything out. You owe a friend fifty dollars? Write out an IOU on a piece of scrap paper. You still owe seventeen dollars on a store credit card that you haven't used in over a year? That counts, too.
- For nonrevolving debt—a mortgage, car payment, hospital bill—one statement should be enough and should contain all the information you need. For revolving credit—those pesky little credit cards—get a year's worth of statements. What you want to see here is not only what you owe but also a clear picture, no matter how ugly, of what you have decided to spend your Monopoly money on.

If you use financial software or have access to your accounts online, gathering a year's worth of statements should be quite easy. But you will likely want to print them out to make it easier to compare them with your other statements.

- Now look through this pile and make a list of the *kinds* of things that you have borrowed money for. The list might look something like this:

SOME THINGS I'VE BOUGHT (AND AM STILL PAYING FOR . . .)

1. a house
2. a trip to Key West
3. over seventy-five dinners out
4. a car
5. ten new pairs of shoes
6. two cell phones
7. tickets to a Knicks game
8. a trip to the emergency room
9. software
10. video games

What you are looking at is a snapshot of both your choices and your circumstances—things that you have decided to spend money on and expenses that may have caught you with your financial pants down.

- Carefully look over this list and your statements. Do this in as analytical a manner as possible, and without judgment. You're not doing it so that you can end up feeling worse about your situation. You are simply looking for patterns. Trends. What do you notice about the things you whipped out the plastic for? Which bills do you feel good about? Bad about? Your emotional reaction to this can tell you a lot.

Remember, these are items that you paid for that you did not have the cash on hand to afford. Was it worth it?

If it was, great. If you hate the idea of continuing to pay 11 percent (or much more) interest on a mediocre meal you ate months ago, consider that reaction valuable information as you make credit choices going forward.

NOT ALL DEBT IS CREATED EQUAL

Good debt, bad debt. Isn't it all the same, your hard-earned money getting sucked out of your accounts? Well, yes and no. Some debts build you up; others tear you down. Some are also assets; others are merely sucking the lifeblood out of you for nothing more than succumbing to Pavlovian consumer triggers. ("Last chance for savings! Limited time only! Buy now, pay later!")

For example: A school loan is not considered bad debt for a couple of reasons. First, education is considered a good investment. Also, you can deduct a portion of the interest you pay each year from your annual taxes, and finally, the percentage rates are relatively low.

ONE BIG, HAPPY BILL . . . .

Many of us accumulated a healthy chunk of debt to further our educations. If you have multiple student loans, you may wish to consider consolidating them. Not only can this lower your rate, but it will improve your mental health to have one bill to pay rather than three (or more). Information about consolidating your loans with the Department of Education can be found here: http://loanconsolidation.ed.gov.

A mortgage is usually considered good debt (provided you didn't take on a mortgage that is beyond your means). Your house—in theory—increases in value. You can live in it. Paying off a mortgage is one of the most empowering, rewarding things you can do. The interest rates can—and should, if you can swing it—be fixed, and the interest paid is tax deductible.

Cars can be a little trickier but are still generally considered not terrible debt to have. Cars are an asset, too. Though their value declines, they will retain some. Cars and houses are also considered "secured" debt—they are secured by the item itself. If you welsh on your loan, the lender can always repo. For this reason, the interest on a car loan is almost always less than what you would pay on a credit card. Is paying your car off a good idea? Yes. Is leasing a brand-new Jag when you clearly make a used-Chevy kind of living a bad idea? Yes again.

So what is bad debt? Just about everything else. As we've said before, the variable earning schedule can plague even the best of freelancers, often leaving them in a situation where their credit card is the only option. But there are emergencies, and then there are . . . you know, denial-laden justifications for why you just have to have something *now*. You slap a new hard drive on the credit card because you can't believe what a fantastic deal you're getting on it. But by the time you've paid it off, it's ended up costing you more than the original presale price. You decide you deserve a vacation—and we agree that you do, you really, really do—but the cost sits on your card for two years and you come back from your time in the sun even more stressed about your quaky-shaky finances than you were before you left. This book is about helping you organize your finances in such a way that there are other options than a nonstop trip to plastic hell. The reason we are having you stare down all those charges on your card(s) is that you cannot create a system that works for you without basing it in reality.

Remember this: credit cards are the dragons of the financial world. Slay them, one by one.

So let's continue dissecting your debt profile. . . .

BREAKING IT DOWN

Now we are going to take that big pile of debt snapshots and separate the lovely little interest-earning gems into separate piles.

STEP 1: PILE IT ON

- *Pile 1.* Put your "good" debt here. Mortgages, student loans, cars.
- *Pile 2.* Credit-card debt. All store and bank credit cards go here. You will be tempted to set this on fire. Be strong.
- *Pile 3.* Everything else. Hospital bills, personal loans from friends or family, any other fixed payments that you are currently paying down.

STEP 2: BY THE NUMBERS

Get out a piece of paper. Write "Good," "Bad," and "Everything Else" across the top of the page. Starting with pile one, write down the following information for each of your debts:

- Who holds it (bank, mortgage company, hospital, etc.)
- The amount owed

- The interest rate
- Any additional relevant information (For example, if you are enjoying a low-interest introductory rate for one of your credit cards, when does that expire? What will the rate be when it does? Write it down.)

STEP 3: RANK 'EM

Now for each list, place your debts in order from highest interest rate to lowest. Be sure to flag any introductory interest rates that are going to expire before you can pay them off. (We will talk about when and how to pay down your debt next.)

A completed list for your credit cards might look something like this:

BAD DEBT

Tarzhay	$874	21%
CitySpank	$2,789	14.3%
Behest Buy	$352	11.9%
First United Impulse	$3,011	0%*

*This rate goes up to 15% in June.

The interest rate is the key to everything. It's all the credit-card companies care about, so it's all you should care about, too.

WHAT TO REDUCE AND WHEN

Now that you have surveyed your debts and ranked them according to the interest rate you are paying on them, you are ready to take the next step. The rationale presented here will form the basis of the payment plan you'll implement when you set up your accounts in part II.

STEP 1: PAY THE MINIMUM ON THE GOOD DEBTS

Unless the interest rates on any of your nonrevolving debts are obscenely high, you will not make them a priority for payoff at this time. Also, the interest rates on the "good" and "everything else" debts are not likely to change. Because card issuers have devoted their lives to creating sneaky little read-the-fine-print ways of jacking up your rates, you have to get rid of these first. You will commit to paying your monthly minimum on the nonrevolving debts until you have expunged the bad.

STEP 2: HIDE THE CARDS

You can't pay off debt if you're still slapping stuff on plastic. You must cease using the cards during the time you are paying them off. We can hear you yelling, "How am I going to live?!" You're going to do it the way your great-great-grandparents did. We will help you set up a small financial cushion to buttress you if you're in trouble. Meanwhile, you'd do well to take all the cards out of your wallet and hide them in their respective folders in your financial file cabinet. (Don't destroy the cards; just hide them.) From this moment forward, until the sweet sunshine of debt freedom kisses your brow, you will commit to paying cash or using your debit cards. We mean it. So get real and commit.

STEP 3: PAY OFF THE BAD DEBTS, TOP TO BOTTOM

Now. Take a gander at your bad debts. Not a pretty sight, is it? Look at the card at the top of the page. This son of a bitch is charging you the most interest, so it must die first. For as long as it takes, you will commit to paying as much money as you can possibly afford to this one card. Meanwhile, you will continue paying the minimum on all the other cards on your list.

ALTERNATE STEP 3: PAY OFF THE BAD DEBTS, SMALLEST AMOUNT FIRST

Sometimes it helps to win a few psychological battles, especially if you've got lots of debt to eradicate. For this reason, you may want to focus on erasing the smallest debt you have first. For example, say you owe a total of $352 to Behest Buy at 11.9 percent interest. It's the smallest amount that you owe on any of your cards, but it has the third-highest interest rate. Strictly speaking, you would be correct to pay it off third, after you slay your top two dragons. But you know you could pay the Behest Buy card off in one month's time, and if you did, you'd feel fantastic. That can mean a lot as you undertake this enormous challenge. Similarly, if you have one of those cards with an introductory, too-good-to-be-true rate that is due to expire soon, you may wish to deviate from your top-to-bottom approach to pay that off before the interest rate heads for the rafters. Then go right back up to the top and work your way down.

STEP 4: PAY, PAY, PAY

There is no easy way to pay off debt. Basically, in the months or years it takes to get rid of all these cards, you will ruthlessly economize to free up every spare dollar you can to pay them off. In chapter 9, we will spell out some creative mathematical fool-yourself strategies that will help you get a jump start and show you how to start paying your debt down in the Freelance Finance system.

STEP 5: STAY MOTIVATED

A wealth of online debt calculators can help you stay pumped as you see your goal through to the end. In an ideal world, you should strive to make payments of 10 percent of your balance to wow the credit agencies. If your balance is ginormous, this may well be impossible. But it's educational to play with calculators, envision various payment scenarios, and see what is possible. Consider: When we plugged in Erin's Target balance, interest rate, and minimum payments, we learned that with minimum payments it would take her more than seven years to pay off the card. And in that time, she would have paid $1,580 in interest, more than half of the original amount she owed. However, if she paid 10 percent of the original amount each month, the debt would be gone in ten easy payments. Go play with calculators! You'll love it. Now, we know that it's not always so easy. Many people are in serious credit-card debt, and even the minimum payments are unmanageable. If this sounds like you, it may be time to seek professional help.

DON'T BE AFRAID TO ASK FOR HELP

Sometimes you just need to know when to say, *You know what? I can't handle this on my own anymore. I need help.* Each year, millions of people do just this: they reach out to credit counselors to help them get the debt monkey off their back.

The reason "drowning" is so often associated with debt is that that's what it feels like: there is an endless sea of paper and obligations that you can't seem to rise above no matter how hard you try. It's suffocating.

One of the benefits of going through counseling is that

instead of feeling alone, you have someone on your team who can help you take on whatever boogeymen might be lurking in your file cabinet. Counselors will advise you, support you, and instruct you on how best to get things under control. If you find yourself in particularly dire straits, you may be able to participate in a more stringent debt-management plan. In most cases, you would make one payment to the counseling service and they, in turn, would distribute the funds to your various unpaid accounts. The counselors will also be able to negotiate a lower interest rate on your behalf. But if you think you get to hold on to your collection of credit cards as part of this plan, think again.

We have listed two resources in the appendix that can help you down the counseling road should you choose to take it. If you decide to look into things on your own, just be careful. Remember that—in tough economic times, especially—there will always be some shady outfit posing as the answer to your fiscal prayers, ready to buy your debt from you, buy your house from you, buy your dog from you. So in short, debtor beware! We strongly suggest you start with the organizations we've listed (no, we don't get anything from them). You want a nonprofit agency that has been around for a while. This shouldn't be hard, as many have been around for decades. And if someone is trying to charge you exorbitant fees for their help, *run away*. Fast. Pack up your statements and hightail it outta there.

OLD-SCHOOL DEBT

In an age when banks are charging other banks 2 percent, more or less, to borrow money, why do credit-card companies get away with charging you 19.9 percent on purchases? Because they can. By law, they are allowed to charge whatever they want, provided they spell out the terms of the card in the fine print you get when you sign up. The new credit-card laws passed in May 2009 have helped, but we would argue that credit-card issuers still hold all the cards, so to speak. They can still increase your rates if you fall behind on your payments.

How can you fight back? Never give them a chance to raise your rates. Get retro on their asses. Our pal Karl, a film producer, loves telling us how his dad has always paid for things in cash. We're talking cars and even houses. This may be too extreme for most pocketbooks, but you get the point. There was a time in this country when average joes were averse to taking on credit. Maybe it's time to start acting with the wisdom of a horn-rimmed midwesterner, circa 1962: Can't afford it? Don't buy it. Want it badly? Save for it.

DEBT = DREAMS DEFERRED

Look at this equation. Read it. Let it sink in. What is disturbing about the times we live in is that there are people everywhere telling you that debt is OK. They speak with great authority, as if to say that whatever you borrow doesn't have to be paid back. There are adjustable rates, introductory offers, deferred payments, buy-now-pay-later deals. Guess what? You eventually pay. Big time. More than the original price, usually.

Case in point: In late 2007, we were approached by a bank "officer" (the guise of authority again) at our bank about this *amazing* opportunity. She pressed us to consider a mortgage that would allow us to pay whatever we wanted toward our home's principal and funnel the rest into a retirement account. Imagine that! Mortgage payments funding our retirement. The catch was that the more money you diverted from your principal, and the more you saved in your retirement fund, *the more you owed on the house.* The idea sounded asinine to us. It seemed strange to think that you would pay, pay, pay your "mortgage" but never actually reduce the principal.

"Not to worry," the bank officer smiled, winked, nodded. "Your house will appreciate, and when you sell it, that will make up for the increase."

After all, she went on, statistically most people live in a home for only seven years anyway, and houses *always* go up in value.

Flash forward six months: The world economy was in total meltdown precisely because of mortgages such as this. One day, we were at the bank to deposit a check. (Let's face it—when those suckers come in, you drop what you're doing to go deposit them.) We *so* wanted to stick our heads in the bank officer's office and give her a big "I told you so."

But she didn't have a job anymore.

In short, people lie. Or, to be more generous, they don't know any better. *Learn to think for yourself.* As the cliché goes, if it sounds too good to be true, it probably is.

We're not going to pull any punches: debt is financial slavery. The sooner you free yourself from it, the more money you will have for your savings, your career, your family, and your dreams.

WHAT TO DO

In this chapter we asked you to get up close and personal with your debt. Drag it out, dust it off, and prepare to kick it in the *tuchas.* Make sure you've done the following:

- Identify and categorize your debt. Examine carefully what you've spent money you didn't have on. Which purchases seemed worth it to you? Which do you regret? (p. 67)

- Rank any credit-card debt you have according to interest rate. (p. 72)

- Have fun with some online debt calculators. We have listed a bunch in the appendix. Put in the amount you owe on a credit card, type in the amount you want to pay, and the magic calculator will tell you how long it will take you to pay the amount off and—here's the important part—how much interest you'll pay, too. (p. 75)

CHAPTER 4

SPENDING MONEY. ON PURPOSE.

Let's be blunt: why on earth are you doing all this?

Why did you buy this book? Why are you taking time away from going out with friends, watching your favorite sitcom, or simply napping, to compile receipts, read about financial calculators, and turn over every rock in an ongoing mission to get a grip on your finances? Seriously—is this what you really want to be doing with your time?

Yes! It's about time you took back the financial night, stopped beating yourself up, and started taking major action on your own behalf. Because you know that your financial well-being is the key to your future, and it's a future that you want to enjoy, to grab hold of, and to ride out for the rest of your days, a sweet smile on your face and some cashola in your pocket.

But getting serious about money isn't just about having money to pay the bills. Sure, bills are part of the equation, especially for those of us who have variable incomes. But to procure wealth, you need a vision. Something to focus on, something that gets you out of bed in the morning and gets you pumped about going through the day and sticking to the commitment you've made to take charge of your finances.

If you're in a creative biz and love what you're doing, that vision might be one of a successful, well-funded business the running of which builds you up, not breaks you down. If you are working part-time jobs on an overtime basis and want to improve your situation and settle your finances, you might envision a life with a new job, a new degree, or a secure retirement. Or maybe it is being able to travel the world or put your kids through college. No matter what your vision, you certainly want to be in a situation where you aren't worried every time a bill comes in the door about whether or not you have the money to cover it. See yourself in your vision. Focus on it. Own it. You're going to live it.

Your complete vision is made up of goals, and they can be big or small, tangible or intangible, short-term or long. Do you want a house? A car? Do you want to sleep the peaceful sleep of those who know their financial duckies are all in a row? Do you want to be able to take vacations on a whim? Or do you simply want to be able to retire someday, before you're ninety?

PRIORITIES: GET THEM STRAIGHT AND MAKE THINGS HAPPEN

To achieve your vision, you have to not only identify your goals but prioritize them as well, according to your ideals and principles. This gives you purpose. It puts you in the driver's seat of a Maserati, rather than feeling like you're stuck on a treadmill going nowhere. Not to veer off into the existential pastures here, but . . . Who are you? What do you stand for? What matters most to you? Simple questions, not-so-simple answers. Working to align your financial goals with the answers to these questions helps you prioritize and makes it easier to head that Maserati in the direction of your vision. Along the way you'll be refining your Spending Identity.

For independent workers, focusing on what truly matters is exceptionally important because we are already facing cash-flow issues, and that unpredictability can make it very hard to zoom in on the long-range vision, because the short-range panic—*Where's my %$***!! check!*—can really get in the way. Also, those of you who have your own businesses and enjoy what you do for a living might not be looking forward to "retiring," per se. Maybe you're more focused on achieving your career goals and you'd be happy to go on working at them forever (though you will likely want to slow down at some point and will need cash set aside to do so).

So brush your teeth, comb your hair, put on your sassiest expression, and take a long gander at your mug in the mirror. Ask that person: What do you want? What do you value most? What are you prepared to do in order to achieve the grand vision you have for your life? The next few sections will help you streamline your answers to those questions.

GETTING DOWN TO BUSINESS

In this chapter, you are going to

- identify your financial goals;
- categorize those goals to look for trends;
- prioritize your goals as a step toward building an action plan.

Our aim here is to make you aware not only of your goals but of whether or not those goals are in line with your personal ideals. In earlier chapters, we had you take a good look at what you were spending your money on and for which purchases you had incurred debt. That same kind of self-analysis will help you here as you lay the foundation for a financial system that serves the specific needs of *your* life—not those of a nine-to-fiver with bennies.

We can hear you already: "I'm mired in debt. I don't know how I'm going to make ends meet this year. How can I possibly think about things I want to achieve financially five, ten, or even twenty years down the road?"

To this we respond: You must think about these things. If you don't, no one else will. And guess what? It's *your* responsibility. If you can think about the future now, no matter what your present circumstances, you will still be in a better position to create that vision down the line. If you are in your twenties or thirties, you are in the ideal position to begin creating a sensible, workable financial life. If you're not—it's never too late to start. Your commitment can only improve your circumstances. Where will you be if you decide it's too late, too hard, too time-consuming? Right where you are. Where will you be if you commit to a new direction? Maybe one step closer to the wheel of that Maserati.

We've already mentioned that goals can be tangible (a house) or intangible (less stress). You are going to focus on the tangible here, and you are going to take those goals and make them even more focused and more tangible—rendering them all the more achievable. And believe us—achieving the tangible brings the intangible within reach, too. For example: if you pay off your credit cards (tangible goal), your desire to feel less stressed about your finances (intangible goal) will be well on its way to being achieved.

START BIG, NARROW IT DOWN

What are your financial goals? If you've never taken the time to think about this before, because you're too busy treading water month to month, this simple question may stump you for a second. The easiest way to find out is to go somewhere alone, sit down with a pencil, and start emptying everything that's rattling around in your noggin onto a piece of paper. This requires a little bit more effort than you may realize because, for whatever reason, all of us have been trained since childhood to focus on material wants, at the expense of deeper, more resonating financial goals. It's not that we won't be discussing material wants here—we want you to. But sit quietly for a few minutes and think about what's really missing from your financial life and what you most desire from your fiscal profile that would set you off in a new, better, healthier direction. If you can be honest with yourself, you may be surprised at what you truly want.

1. LIST THE WANTS

You can write your list any way you like, but we'd love it if you could stick to two basic rules:

1. Be as specific as possible.
2. Make sure each line that you write contains a verb.

For now, don't bother trying to organize your list in any particular way. Just jot down whatever comes to mind. If you have to go over your list a second or third time to fiddle with the language so it manages to adhere to our rules, that's fine.

When you're done, your list might look something like the

one shown below. Don't worry if your list is three, five, or ten times longer—or a little shorter. It's perfectly OK.

WHAT I WANT

I want to pay off my credit card.

I want to pay off my car.

I want to have at least one nice vacation at the beach every year for the rest of my life.

I want to have health insurance.

I want to save for retirement.

I want my business to make enough to support me and two other employees.

I want to donate to my favorite charity.

I want to be able to eat out more.

I want new clothes for work.

I want to buy a house.

I want to pay for my wedding.

I want enough money for a gym membership.

I want a kayak.

I want a digital SLR camera.

I want to rent an office for my business.

I want to go back to school and get my degree.

I want to travel more.

I want to put solar panels on my roof.

2. CATEGORIZE THE WANTS

A list such as this is illuminating, but it quickly becomes unmanageable if you don't take steps to organize it. What's more important, the kayak or paying off the credit-card bills?

If you're getting married in the next year, isn't that more of a priority than renting office space? In order to make this list useful to you, you've got to break it down and group common wants together under a larger category or theme. For example, our sample list has a bunch of things, objects, or stuff that would all fall into the category of "material goods." We're willing to bet that your list has quite a few material desires on it, too. Don't be ashamed of that. Nearly everyone who does this exercise is going to have a bunch of material goods on their list. It's just human nature. So without making any kind of judgment about it, go ahead and take out another sheet of paper. On this piece of paper you are going to list the categories of all your wants. Start by writing "Material Goods" across the top and then listing the wants that fall into that category beneath that heading, as shown here and on page 87.

MATERIAL GOODS

I want a kayak.

I want a digital SLR camera.

I want new clothes for work.

Then go on to group the other wants on your list into a variety of other categories. If you have trouble coming up with categories, here's a hint: they tend to be nouns. Words like "creativity," "leisure," "financial security," "family," "health," "home," "education," and "public service" all make great categories.

Get to work now. Go down your wants list, dreaming up categories that seem to grow naturally from each of your wants. Jot the themes on your sheet of paper and list the appropriate wants under each category heading. (You will find a blank chart that you can fill in on your own on page 92. Photocopy as needed.) Revise these lists as necessary. Once you're looking at the big picture, you may need to move some things around. We will show you how shortly.

When you're done, your list of categories and corresponding wants might look something like this:

WHAT I WANT

~~MATERIAL GOODS~~

~~I want a kayak.~~

~~I want a digital SLR camera.~~

~~I want new clothes for work.~~

FINANCIAL SECURITY

I want to pay off my credit card.

I want to pay off my car.

I want to have health insurance.

I want to save for retirement.

LEISURE

I want to have at least one nice vacation at the beach every year for the rest of my life.

I want to be able to eat out more.

I want to travel more.

I want a kayak.

I want a digital SLR camera.

~~BUSINESS~~ ~~SUCCESS~~ CAREER

I want my business to make enough to support me and two other employees.

I want to rent an office for my business.

I want to go back to school and get my degree.

I want new clothes for work.

PUBLIC SERVICE

I want to donate to my favorite charity every year.

HOME

I want to buy a house.

I want to put solar panels on my roof.

FAMILY

I want to pay for my wedding.

HEALTH

I want enough money for a gym membership.

You'll notice three things about this list of our categories and corresponding wants:

1. It turned out that the material goods on our list really *did* fit reasonably well into two of our other categories. As we were working, we realized that the kayak and camera wants actually grew out of our desire to travel and see the world. Be open to the possibility that a material good without a related category might need to be deleted.

2. It took us three tries before we nailed down the name of the fourth category. Now it feels just right. You shouldn't be afraid to keep revising your categories until they work for you, too.

3. It helps to have as few categories as possible. How few? Five or six would be ideal. *A short list is a manageable list.* Our current list has seven. We could probably compress further, by combining "home" and "family." Do whatever feels best for you.

3. RANK THE WANTS

We want you to achieve and obtain every single thing you've listed here. But let's be frank—you will likely not get to have them all at once. So within each category, rank what you've listed according to how important the items feel to you. This is a critical step. If you are dealing with limited funds, you are going to have to make some choices about where to direct them. There's no getting around that. Purposeful spending is smart spending. If you feel that it might help you think more clearly about everything, you may wish to prioritize the categories as well. Look at page 90 to see how we ranked some of the items on our final lists.

WHAT I WANT

FINANCIAL SECURITY

1. I want to have health insurance.
2. I want to save for retirement.
3. I want to pay off my credit card.
4. I want to pay off my car.

CAREER

1. I want to go back to school and get my degree.
2. I want to rent an office for my business.
3. I want my business to make enough to support me and two other employees.
4. I want new clothes for work.

LEISURE

1. I want to be able to eat out more.
2. I want to have at least one nice vacation at the beach every year for the rest of my life.
3. I want to travel more.
4. I want a digital SLR camera.
5. I want a kayak.

PUBLIC SERVICE

1. I want to donate to my favorite charity every year.

HOME AND FAMILY

1. I want to pay for my wedding.
2. I want to buy a house.
3. I want to put solar panels on my roof.

HEALTH

1. I want enough money for a gym membership.

It's easy to see how this list could serve as a kind of blueprint for future financial planning. Anyone looking at this list could quickly determine what you stand for. Principles, values, or morals—whatever you want to call them—these themes summarize what you hope to achieve with money in your life. Before you move on to the next step, look them over. Do these groups provide an accurate picture of your financial priorities? Do you read this list and say, *Absolutely; that's me in a nutshell; that's what's important to me today*?

Or do you look at these and think, *Huh. Well, I don't really care as much about the kayak as I do about the health insurance. What materialistic idiot came up with this list, anyway?* If that is the case, don't beat yourself up. There's nothing wrong with wanting the kayak. Just know that your health insurance takes priority. (And know this before you whip out the plastic demon.) So if you feel the categories and priorities listed don't quite paint an accurate picture of who you are—or, rather, who you want to be—then maybe you want to take some more time to nail down a list that you're more comfortable with.

Start by writing your wants on another sheet or sheets of paper. When you're ready, use this sheet to start organizing your lists.

YOUR WANTS AND CATEGORIES LIST

CATEGORY: ______________________________

Want: ______________________________

Want: ______________________________

Want: ______________________________

Want: ______________________________

Want: ______________________________

CATEGORY: ______________________________

Want: ______________________________

Want: ______________________________

Want: ______________________________

Want: ______________________________

Want: ______________________________

CATEGORY: ______________________________

Want: ______________________________

Want: ______________________________

Want: ______________________________

Want: ________________________________

Want: ________________________________

CATEGORY: ________________________________

Want: ________________________________

Want: ________________________________

Want: ________________________________

Want: ________________________________

Want: ________________________________

CATEGORY: ________________________________

Want: ________________________________

Want: ________________________________

Want: ________________________________

Want: ________________________________

Want: ________________________________

4. GET SPECIFIC

When you're ready, look at the top five goals in each category. If you want to achieve these, it's best to get specific. In other words, you'll need to spell out the details and related costs of what it will take to make any one of these items come true. Why do we need to take the time to get specific? Why ruin these wonderful dreams by subjecting them to a cold blast of reality? Because otherwise, you can't really plan for any of these things and take action to achieve or obtain them.

Look at it this way. Say one night you go out to eat at a fancy restaurant. Candles on the table. Linen napkins. Flowers. The whole bit. The waiter hands you the menu and your eyes alight on a wonderful description of a juicy salmon steak. *I want that!* you tell yourself.

After a few minutes, the waiter comes by. "What will you have this evening?" he asks.

"I'll have the fish," you say.

A little while later, the waiter returns with a covered dish and whips off the lid. *Voilà!* There on the platter before you is a beautiful dish of . . . fish and chips.

Ugh. What happened? You didn't spell out exactly what you wanted. If you're not clear about what you want, don't be surprised if you're leading a fish-and-chips life when you really want a salmon-steak future.

Don't let this happen to you.

Work through each of the items on your list. (There's a worksheet on page 97 to help you do this.)

- Research what it would cost to make each of these things come true.
- Wherever possible, spell out costs and dates.
- To simplify your work, you may wish to focus on all the number one items on your list. Or some people prefer to tackle a category—financial security, for example. Pick an approach and go for it.

Here's how you might recast your original statements to be more specific.

Original statement: "I want to save for retirement."
Specific statement: "I want to have five hundred thousand dollars combined in a Roth IRA and SEP by the time I'm 50 years old."

Original statement: "I want new clothes for work."
Specific statement: "I want to buy one new suit, two pairs of shoes, and three new outfits in the next six months. I will need a total of $2,500 to make this happen."

Original statement: "I want to pay off my credit card."
Specific statement: "I want to have a zero balance on my credit card within two years. I will need to pay $182 a month to make this happen."

Original statement: "I want to travel more."
Specific statement: "I want to travel around Central America for two weeks. A package deal costs $3,100."

It's important to verify what these wants will cost you. You will carry those numbers with you into part II and plug them into the system. In most cases, your "research" will consist of simply figuring out what something costs and writing it down. A little digging online will tell you that the new camera you want will cost $680.

But some of your statements will require more research. Let's look at one of the examples above. If one of your wants is to pay off your credit card within two years, and your balance is currently $3,749, you'll need to use a credit-card-payoff calculator (like the one at dinkytown.net) to run the numbers. In this way, you'll learn that your 14.9 percent credit card can be paid off in twenty-four months if you can manage to pay $182 a month.

No matter the goal, you can usually reduce the big total to a monthly figure. That way, you can quickly see whether that number fits into your budget or Spending Identity. Don't get overwhelmed. If you run the numbers on your five-hundred-thousand-dollar retirement fund, you may be tempted to say, *Oh, my God—there's no way I can save for this.*

Don't look at what you can't do; look at what you *can* do. Maybe you can't save for a house *and* pay down your huge credit-card balance *and* save for Central America all at the same time. But you *can* save or pay a little toward each or decide to focus on one goal before moving on to the next. (And it pays to be repetitive here: if you have unruly credit-card debt, your best bet is to start there.)

People shy away from specificity because they're in love with the idea of dreams staying forever intangible, ethereal "dreams." *Hey,* they think, *if I can't put a price tag on my dreams, they can't be grounded in reality, and therefore I never have to realistically save for them.* On the other hand, once you put a price tag on the thing you desire most, once you reduce it to a monthly cost, you will quickly grasp the amount of sacrifice and commitment that needs to go into it. Sure, the trip sounds like more fun. But what is more important to you, financial security or leisure? Only you can answer that question.

Prioritizing your dreams is a powerful process. It may be that once you know the hard mathematical facts, you'll realize that some of your lesser goals aren't really worth the effort. Either you'll scratch them off entirely or you'll simply kick them further down the list.

Research what it will cost to achieve each of your wants. Rewrite them again, using more specific financial language.

THE GET-SPECIFIC SHEET

CATEGORY: ______________________________

Specific Want: ______________________________

Specific Want: ______________________________

Specific Want: ______________________________

Specific Want: ______________________________

Specific Want: ______________________________

CATEGORY: ______________________________

Specific Want: ______________________________

Specific Want: ______________________________

Specific Want: ______________________________

Specific Want: ______________________________

Specific Want: ______________________________

CATEGORY: ______________________________

Specific Want: ______________________________

Specific Want: ______________________________

Specific Want: ______________________________

Specific Want: ______________________________

Specific Want: ______________________________

CATEGORY: ____________________

Specific Want: ____________________

Specific Want: ____________________

Specific Want: ____________________

Specific Want: ____________________

Specific Want: ____________________

CATEGORY: ____________________

Specific Want: ____________________

Specific Want: ____________________

Specific Want: ____________________

Specific Want: ____________________

Specific Want: ____________________

YOUR LIFESTYLE, YOUR LIFE

We know it feels a little hokey to make these kinds of lists, but unless you create them, you might very well keep your real dreams—the ones that lurk beneath the shiny new toys—squirreled away inside you, never to see the light of day. Or worse, you'll express them in weird, chaotic ways.

Telling yourself what you want, announcing it, seems to have a power all its own.

When Joe was still living with a roommate, he wanted nothing more than to have enough money for a down payment on a condo of his own. He longed for his own space, his own home.

Since he liked to cook, he dreamed that someday, when he had his own place, he would cook up fantastic meals day and night.

Or so went the fantasy.

But his desire for his own place got melded in his confused little head with having a well-stocked kitchen. Instead of announcing his specific want to himself and making a financial plan to save for a down payment, he spent lavishly on handsome copper pots, baking molds, and dozens of knickknacky kitchen utensils, packing them into his already cramped, shared kitchen. Around the time he bought a ninety-dollar chinoise—which is nothing more than a fancy strainer—he snapped out of it and realized: this is not saving for a house. Seriously, unless he's Jamie Oliver, a man in his thirties doesn't really *need* a chinoise.

Joe was *surrogate spending*—trading associated but meaningless short-term spending for a more important long-term goal. Why? He hadn't categorized and prioritized his financial goals. If he had, he would have realized that the condo was the priority and that the money he was spending to *feel* like he had the kitchen of his dreams could have been going toward actually securing that future for himself.

Once he got real, he was in a place of his own within a couple of years.

Spelling out what you want collapses the amount of time you need to wait for it. It's the shortcut to all-too-tangible dreams.

SPEAK UP!

If you wanted to run for office, which would have more impact: thinking about it, silently deciding that you wanted to do it, or announcing to voters that you intended to run? The last, of course. But you would have to be sure, right? Because once you say something out loud, once you put something out there, you are on the hook for it. It becomes much, much harder to back out.

The same is true of committing to life-changing habits. Ask anyone who has tried to quit something (smoking, drinking, eating fast food) or start something (a new exercise regime, a novel). There is power in numbers, there is strength in support, and there is major muscle in accountability. For this reason, it is key that you take steps to announce your goals loudly, publicly. Write them down. Commit to them. Say them out loud. Tell a friend. Better yet, join a group. The blogosphere has lots of interesting sites, such as Debt Kid (debtkid.com), Blogging Away Debt (bloggingawaydebt.com), and Money Funk (moneyfunk.net), where people just like you are writing about getting their financial lives on track.

It's even more important to stick to your guns when you're not with like-minded folks. Make a point, the next time someone suggests a high-end restaurant instead of your usual dive or mentions the possibility of a road trip to the beach for a long weekend, of using the opportunity to announce your intention to live in support of your financial priorities. But choose your words carefully. Don't say "I can't afford ______." Instead, start your response with "I'm saving to buy . . ." Or simply say, "Sorry, no, I've committed to paying down my credit card."

This is not really about being able to afford something. It's about choosing, wisely, how you want to spend your money. So no matter where you look for support or how you seize opportunities to announce your newfound financial fortitude, make your intentions known. Independent workers of the world, unite! Trust us—you'll feel better, and you'll succeed faster.

PART I: RECAP

Before we dive headlong into the heart of the Freelance Finance system, let's take a look at what you've done so far:

- You have resolved to get serious about your finances.
- You have organized your financial files.
- You have committed to educating yourself about personal finance.
- You have assessed and analyzed your earning history, your fixed monthly costs, and your discretionary spending.
- You have come to better understand your Spending Identity.
- You have examined your debt profile and examined the situations that have caused you to become indebted.
- You have ranked your debts according to their interest rates.
- You have listed and prioritized your financial goals and have determined the cost of achieving those that mean the most to you.

Congratulations! So now what, you say? You will take all of this hard work and valuable information and learn to integrate them into a financial plan that works for you, the independent worker. Regardless of how much you earn, how much you owe, how much you save, or where you spend it, you are about to make strides toward the financial future you have always wanted and dreamed of.

WHAT TO DO

- Describe your vision. Write out, longhand, what your ideal financial life looks like and how it fits into the rest of your world. Be as specific as you can.

- List all of your wants. Categorize them. Rank them. Now think long and hard about your ideals, the things that matter most to you. Does this list reflect those values? (p. 84)

- Announce your intention to live a life that is more in line with your financial goals. Share this with someone who will help keep you accountable. (p. 99)

PART II

THE BASICS OF THE SYSTEM

If you would be wealthy, think of saving as well as getting.

—BENJAMIN FRANKLIN

You now know a little bit more about your earning and spending trends. You have a clearer idea of your weaknesses and strengths. You have looked your finances right in the eye and seen the good as well as the hairy, ugly, and out of control. Now you're going to seize control of the whole shebang.

You're going to make that money work for you. Or you'll be a slave to it for the rest of your life.

CHAPTER 5

AN INTRODUCTION TO THE SYSTEM

A friend of ours started a summer camp program in California. Sid poured every ounce of his determination and love into this program. In organizing this program, he first figured out how much he needed to charge in order to cover the expenses and pay himself a salary for the time invested. Smart. But when the payments started rolling in, he took all of the tuition money and put it in one account. The teenagers arrived, the fun began, and Sid started taking money out of the account in order to cover everything from meals to car rentals and sightseeing excursions. By the time the campers were ready to head home, their adventure had been a resounding success. But unfortunately, along the way, Sid had spent all of his profit. Downtrodden by the sobering fact that all his efforts had paid off in every way except financially, he debated whether or not to continue the program in coming years.

What happened to Sid is not unusual, especially for people who run their own businesses, no matter how small. Specifically, he did three things wrong:

- He budgeted poorly.
- He didn't pay himself first, based on the profit he anticipated earning.

- He put all the money in one account, where earnings and nonstop incidentals mingled until there was nothing left over.

When you run out of money, despite the best intentions and careful planning, the easiest and most common reaction is *Duh, I need more money.* And sure, we would all like more money. But that is not always the answer. Either you didn't plan all that well from the get-go, without specific allocations for needs and expenses, or like our friend, you didn't follow your plan all the way through, down to the very last dollar.

It's difficult to stick to a financial plan without a clear, prioritized approach. It's not enough to do the work and earn the money, only to abandon it in your checking account. You must separate your intended savings from your intended expense money. And you must sock away and separate the savings according to your priorities. Otherwise, the money is not going to end up where you want it. It will just end up spent.

So protect it. One way to do this is to use a system that promotes consciously saving and spending money based on the priorities that you yourself identified. (You did, right? In the last chapter? OK. Just checking . . .)

Think about it: Say you were eating cereal right out of the box (come on . . . we all have) and you wanted to save exactly three-quarters of a cup of it for breakfast the following day, half a cup for your sister's breakfast, and yet another one-third of a cup for a recipe that you intended to try. You are famished—really stuffing it in—and all the while wondering, *Hmmmm . . . How will I know when to stop?* And the chance is pretty good, obviously, that you will eat into some of what you had originally intended to save for later. In this example, the smarter and more obvious thing to do would be to take out the three-quarters of a cup and half a cup and one-third of a cup *before* you start chowing down, right? It's the same with your money. Most of us have ravenous appetites for spending. You need to protect the bucks that need protecting before you consume them in one big gulp. Once you've taken out what you have designated for the future, you can eat to your heart's delight, without worries.

So it's very possible that you don't need more money. (Or maybe you do. Following this system will help you determine if that is, in fact, the case.) We posit that maybe all you need is to work more efficiently with the money you have—make it work for you. This kind of clarity about what you make and where it's going will provide you the ability not only to establish a healthy financial foundation but to better assess your overhead and earning potential, the kinds of things you need to have a good grip on if you want a successful business and some peace of mind. It's not just about *having* money, but about setting it aside for specific goals.

KEYS TO THE SYSTEM

Setting aside money for items that are not only important (retirement) but that can also come back and bite you in the you-know-what if you don't plan for them (taxes) is even more important for freelancers. Why? Because no one else is going to do it for you.

The three basic keys to the system are very straightforward:

- The creation of separate accounts keyed to major financial goals

- The establishment of percentages associated with each of those accounts
- A commitment to consistently pay into these accounts *first*—before money goes out the door for your fixed monthly costs and discretionary spending.

The accounts and percentages are chosen *by you,* based on *your priorities* and the specific needs of your independent working situation. This will not only focus your earning toward your goals, but it will make spending a more relaxed experience. Details about setting up your accounts and percentages will be covered in the next few chapters. For now—because we know you want it—here is a detailed explanation of why this approach works.

POWER OF FOCUSED SPENDING AND SAVING

The accounts you are going to set up will allow you to save for what's important, spend on what matters to you, and to do it all on a regular, habit-forming basis. Habits are not only a hard thing to break, but they are also a hard thing to form. That's why sticking to this plan is key if you're going to make it work—you have to make it a part of your day-to-day relationship with money. All the work you did in part I had a purpose. Really. You are going to tie your accounts back to the priorities you set (with a few suggestions from us, of course). And you are going to stop mixing your apples and oranges and bring an end to those nondescript, generic "savings" accounts. When it comes to your prosperity, commingling funds is the kiss of death.

If you ask someone to list their dreams—or at least those that are going to cost some money—you'll probably get a long list. Most people create long lists in chapter 3. So why, then, when "saving," do so many people have only *one* savings account? How on earth can you keep it all straight? Where does saving for vacation end and saving for retirement begin? That's a lot of cereal that can accidentally get eaten.

One of the simpler and more delightfully retro strategies we can think of—and a prime example of both saving for a purpose and how a little can add up to a lot—is the good ol' Christmas Club. With roots that can be traced as far back as the early 1900s, the Christmas Club really took off during the Great Depression and was still going strong and quite fashionable in the seventies. It is a very simple concept: the Christmas Club is a specialized savings account designed to help folks save up for Christmas presents throughout the year so that they don't get snowed under by debt during the holiday season. Although you don't often hear about it anymore, many banks and credit unions still offer this saving vehicle. We remember the cute little green savings passbook with the red tree on it, our mothers dutifully setting aside just dollars a week. And you know what? Even today, if you were to set aside ten dollars a week starting in January, you would have more than $450 to spend when the holidays rolled around—and none of it would go on your credit card.

WHY PERCENTAGES MAKE SENSE

When they see the word "percentage," some people drop to the floor, snap into a fetal position, and shriek, "No! Please! Not math! Anything but math!" Well, this is both simple and easy. (Please—calculators do the math.) So you can get up off the floor now, pull yourself together, and keep reading.

So why percentages? Because, they are the best—and really only—way to save consistently based on what you actually earn, especially when what you earn varies widely and doesn't arrive on a predictable schedule. Saving a fixed amount on a regular basis—setting up a monthly hundred-dollar withdrawal for your savings, for example—makes sense if you always know when checks are coming in and how much they are going to be worth.

But for independent workers, that doesn't work very well. Many of us have tried this, setting aside a fixed amount every month or from every paycheck, but in the end we were saving either too much when checks were late or too little when things were going well. There is no consistency and no focus (not to mention not enough savings).

That's why we choose to focus on percentages. This is what an employer does, after all. If you have ever had a job where they took out money for taxes or benefits such as a 401(k), perhaps you took the time to look at how much they were taking out of your paycheck. Was it a flat amount? No. Each deduction was a distinct percentage. Think about it: when the feds reach in your pocket for your taxes, they are not in there to pull out some arbitrary amount; they are taking a percentage. Basically, anyone who gets their grubby little hands on your money before you do is looking for a percentage—just like an agent or a bookie. Percentages are the ultimate tool for accumulation.

So we, as responsible independent workers, have to do exactly the same thing. Remember our motto (all together now): treat yourself the way a good employer would treat you. Imagine a world in which you had—gasp!—a generous, caring employer. That employer would be siphoning off a certain percentage of each of your paychecks to pay your taxes, to invest in your retirement fund, and possibly to ensure your health insurance. Since self-employed workers don't usually have such employers, we must spring into action and become our own benevolent sugar daddy (or mama). Yes, this sounds daunting, but freelancers already have something the average cubicle inhabitant may not have: discipline.

We, Joe and Denise, both worked at a children's math magazine back in the day. We were the math geeks at the publishing company. Whenever anyone at any of the other publications had a math question, they came our way. "I got a three percent raise. How much bigger will my paycheck be?" So we "did the math," as it were, for everyone. And then we decided that it was high time that we started doing that with our own accounts. And from this point forward, that's exactly what you're going to do, too.

For example: Let's say you made $43,000 last year, and the money arrived in fifteen checks of varying amounts, ranging from $75 to $8,000. You decided to sock away $50 for every paycheck that came in the door, and you did—congrats. Now, at the end of the year, you had $750. Not bad. But what if you had decided to save a mere 3 percent of each check that came in? By the end of the year you would have had $1,290 saved. Not only that, but the money saved would have reflected what came in the door. When that $75 check arrived, sending $50 right back out the door was probably pretty painful. If you had decided to stick with percentages, you would have parted with only $2.25. And that $8,000 check? Does fifty bucks really sound like a good savings from an $8,000 payday? At 3 percent, it would have been $240. Manageable but equitable. And what if, the following year, you make roughly the same amount of money but it arrives in only eight paychecks? Are you only going to save $400? So you see, with percentages, you are always saving a consistent amount, and it adjusts to the variability of both your schedule and your income.

Are you convinced yet? We'll mention one more thing.

We know what you're thinking: *If I don't know what I'm going to make in a given year, how can I know what kind of percentage to take out?* True, on January 1, most of us don't know what we're going to make in the coming year. But maybe we have a good idea (based on past tax returns, like the ones you examined in chapter 2), or maybe we're just terrified and completely clueless because we have never been in this situation before or are contemplating going out on our own for the first time ever. (Congratulations! Welcome to the clan!) In any case, we will help you choose a percentage to start with.

The only way to maneuver this somewhat tricky financial labyrinth is to take the same percentage out of each check that comes in the door, no matter how big or small, and make sure those percentages are assigned to the most important financial priorities in your life at the moment. And you will do this, without fail, for the rest of your life. No matter what. So when a big check comes in, the amount you set aside will be more than when a small check comes in, but *something*—and something consistent—will always be put toward building your financial security.

ABOUT PAYING YOURSELF FIRST

In 1926, a collection of parables by George Clason was published, titled *The Richest Man in Babylon.* Clason was a businessman—and the first person to publish a road atlas of the United States. He was fascinated with thrift and penned various pamphlets and papers about how to save, setting all of his tantalizing tales of thriftitude in none other than Babylon. Clason is often credited with popularizing the notion that you should pay yourself first, before anyone else. He knew what many of our parents, grandparents, and great-grandparents knew: if you don't pay yourself first, you probably won't do it at all.

We know that money sitting in your checking account is just dying to be spent on downloads and DVDs, dinners out and the babysitters that go along with them. And that is OK, but *only* after you've already scooped up your percentages and sent them on their way to a land of savings or *properly prioritized* spending. Say you want to spend the money for a very noble reason—a huge payment toward your credit-card balance, perhaps—we applaud the instinct. However, by not saving for your taxes, for example, things can turn out to be just as bad—even worse—than if you'd blown that money on a night on the town. Because if you don't have the bucks come April, you will very likely end up slapping that money—and more—right back on the credit card anyway.

With this plan, the accounts you set up will make it clearer and easier not only to pay yourself a percentage first but to pay that percentage where you need it most.

NOT JUST SEPARATE. *DEDICATED.*

Most of you, after completing this book, will have a lot more bank accounts than when you started. And hopefully, you'll be on your way to socking away more money in them, too.

A lot of people with anemic savings have just two accounts: a checking and a savings account. Everyone knows how the checking account works. You write a check or swipe your debit card, and the money flies out of the account. But the savings account is far more amorphous, more elusive. In fact, we can barely hear the phrase anymore without immediately asking the question, "Savings for what?"

Get this, people: *a savings account without a dedicated purpose is unlikely to be fed!*

The way we see it, nobody ever has just a single need to save money. We have multiple needs and goals. Independent workers, of course, have lots to save for that other folks don't have to think about. Taxes are a biggie. Emergencies are, too. (More on both of these in the next chapter.) Ultimately, only you can decide how many accounts you'll need.

Humor us for a second. Say you had ten important categories in your life for which you needed to save. Your taxes. Your retirement. A new car. A child's schooling. Health care. And on and on. Why couldn't you open ten different accounts to serve each of these needs? What the hell is wrong with that? *Absolutely nothing.* And yet people tend to resist doing this because they think it's complicated or troublesome or just plain weird. If they're old enough, they may even think opening multiple bank accounts these days means having to physically visit the bank, talk to a bank officer, fill out forms, copy their driver's license . . .

What's more, some banks levy outrageous fees or refuse to pay you interest if you don't maintain a certain balance in your accounts. Open ten accounts at one of these banks and you'll likely go broke shelling out fees. Sad to say, most of these banks are the brick-and-mortar banks just around the corner from your home. The cost of maintaining a physical location and paying salaries and benefits to their tellers and officers is absolutely reflected in the pathetic interest rates they pay and the irritating minimum balances they demand.

But after you're through reading this book, we hope you'll understand that you have a better choice than to exclusively patronize banks like these. We don't want to judge them too harshly, because they do have their uses. (In fact, our system requires that you have one checking account at a brick-and-mortar bank. More on that later.) We just don't think brick-and-mortars are a good deal for the majority of the saving that independent workers need to do.

Think about it:

- if your income is variable . . .
- if there are long periods when you don't receive a paycheck . . .
- if there's a chance your account balance will drop seriously low . . .

then a bank that demands a high minimum opening deposit or a sizable minimum balance cannot be your primary savings institution. So forget it. That is so 1992. Happily, we and other independent workers now live in an era of convenient online banking. Open one account, and you can instantly open as many additional accounts as you like, completely free.

ABOUT "WEB-ONLY" BANKS

Chances are, if you ask your brick-and-mortar bank if they have an online presence, they'll say, "Absolutely! You can do all your banking from our Web site!"

Unfortunately, that's not what we mean.

By our definition, an online or "Web-only" bank is one whose *primary* retail identity exists in the world of the Internet. (We list a couple of these banks in the appendix.) We like these banks for a few reasons:

- You can open accounts with deposits as little as zero to one dollar.
- They require little to no minimum balance.
- They tend to pay higher interest than brick-and-mortar banks, all the time, regardless of your balance.
- You can open as many accounts as you want at little or no additional cost.
- Your money's safe and FDIC insured.
- You can rename your accounts.
- Withdrawing your money is just tricky enough to keep you from raiding your account and going on a spending spree.

Jeez, when you consider this list, going with an Internet bank is a no-brainer, even for traditionally employed people. But such banks are perfect for people like you, mostly because of the last two attributes on our list. Let's take a look at them.

RENAMING ACCOUNTS

All this means is that you'll be able to click on the number of a savings account and change that number to a written name.

The next time you visit your accounts, instead of seeing a line of nine or so digits, such as "1234567–12," you'll see a highly personal moniker, such as "Brenda's Prius," "My Beach House Rental Fund," or "Getting My Education." Precise names give you a financial clarity that you cannot get from looking at a long list of numbers. Instead of just looking at your accounts, you are looking at your goals. Hey—you sort your e-mails according to senders or projects. Why wouldn't you do the same thing when sorting your funds?

TRICKY WITHDRAWALS

We don't want to give the impression that withdrawing money from an online bank is cumbersome. Far from it. It's just that if you want to access the money in your account, you often have to transfer it to a brick-and-mortar institution first, and then access the money from an ATM in that bank's network. Most Internet banks now give you the option to get an ATM card, but we *strongly* advise you to decline that option. Decline. Decline. Decline. We're serious about this. If you want to be an independent worker who builds wealth, you've got to say "hands off" to the dedicated sums of your money. Don't worry about it. You won't miss it. The way we'll have you up and running, you won't need that cash for your day-to-day life, anyway.

You don't have to open an account just yet; we'd prefer that you learned more about the system first. So for now, do some research. Look at the banks we recommend in the appendix, or look up others at Bankrate.com. Specifically, seek banks that meet all the criteria we listed. If you're not sure if a bank allows you to rename an account or meets any of the other criteria, call it and ask. It's entirely possible that your current brick-and-mortar will do this and more. If so, congratulations. You've got a great bank.

Some of you may feel bad about ditching a bank that employs and services your community. First, we did not say you would never need a brick-and-mortar bank ever again. You do need at least one account in one of these places. Second, get over it. After the federal bailout of 2008–9, American banks have gotten more than their fair share of your money, your children's, and your grandchildren's. It's time to look out for yourself.

WHAT TO EXPECT FROM THE NEXT FEW CHAPTERS

For the next four chapters, we are going to walk you through the following:

- the creation of your savings accounts
- the calculation of the appropriate percentages to assign to each of your accounts
- the step-by-step motions you will go through every time a check comes in the door

Along the way, you will be constantly restructuring your Spending Identity so that it not only matches your reality but is also in line with your financial goals.

Here you have it: You have pored over your financial history, as painful as that may have been. You have assessed your earnings, your fixed income, and your debt. You have brainstormed and analyzed your goals. Now you have begun to examine the logic of separate savings accounts and have come to understand the power of percentages.

You are ready to start feeding your monkey.

WHAT TO DO

Now we are getting right down to the nitty-gritty of things. To prepare for the next section, do the following. Do not move on until you have finished. We're watching. . . .

- Research online banks and choose one where you would like to keep your various savings accounts. (pp. 115–16)
- Revisit your estimated earnings from chapter 2. Look at what you've earned in the past and what you predict—to the extent that you can—that you will earn this year. (p. 41)
- Look at your overhead—the fixed monthly costs that you gathered in chapter 2. Ask yourself again—do these costs seem to match my income? (p. 46)
- Choose your top three financial goals from the lists you created in chapter 4. Write them down. Wait one day. Then go back to your original lists and pick your top three again. Did you pick the same three goals? If not, repeat and revise your short list until you're sure you've keyed in to what's most important to you. (p. 84)

CHAPTER 6

THE HOLY TRINITY OF SAVINGS

A dancer-turned-physical-therapist named Carol told us recently that she had started giving her kids, ages five and seven, an allowance. They received four quarters each. By parental decree, each child had to deposit one quarter into a glass jar earmarked for a local charity. Next, each of them was instructed to drop a second quarter into their own jar marked "Savings."

At this point, after watching two of his quarters disappear, the five-year-old boy asked, "But what's for keepings?"

From that moment on, the family started calling the last two quarters the keepings. Besides this money, the kids could earn a quarter or two more by doing some small chores around the house.

This got us thinking back to our own allowances, paper routes, babysitting—and our own long-gone quarters. How much would we have now if we had saved 25 percent of everything we made back then? How enriched would our favorite charities be if we had happily given them 25 percent from childhood on? And what about the all-important 50 percent in "keepings"? How long did we actually keep that money, and what did we buy with it that we could lay our hands on today?

Now let's turn the question around: imagine saving and investing 50 percent of every dollar you make. That's right—half. Could you do it? We know: it seems virtually impossible. For most of us, saving even 10 percent seems like an enormous commitment. But you have to start somewhere.

We don't care how much you make; the only way to get ahead is to start dropping quarters in that jar. This can be harder for the independent worker. Not knowing precisely what you're making and when it's coming in makes it tricky to set a dollar amount and sock it away weekly or monthly. But what we *can* do is choose a percentage and take that off the top of every check that comes in. Most people need to start small—say, 5 percent. If even that scares the pants off you, start with 3 or even 1 percent. The amount should be so little that you don't even notice it. *Just start.* Then every couple of months, increase that percentage gradually to whatever you think you can stand.

People in the arts always dream of the big score. The high-priced gallery show. One's own dance studio. The big break on the screen. For others, the dream is a thriving business or the Daddy Warbucks repeat clients. Good. We should dream. We should believe.

But the biggest score we've got is the one we're handed every day. We just don't see it. Saving a quarter seems insignificant when we have all these miserable bills to pay—and it should. Still, when you're not looking, those quarters turn into something much more valuable than candy, comic books, and ringtones. A buck a week in childhood could turn into $2,500 by the time you're twenty, $6,300 by the time you're thirty, and $14,500 by the time you're forty years old. You might scoff because the numbers seem small. But would you turn down $2,500 right now?

Most adults remember having some sort of piggy bank. For many of us it was our first experience with saving. We filled our pig, jar, or shoebox with whatever we could scrape together. A few bucks from a friendly relative, some chores, maybe a little babysitting—the next thing you knew, the bank got heavier and heavier until, one day, you tipped that baby over and could hardly believe how much was inside. Here's the thing: savings sneak up on you.

In addition to all of our ranting about the joys of online banking, we still have our monkey bank at home. While we like pumping dimes and quarters into our monkey, he has come to represent much more than just a belly full of spare change. The idea of feeding the monkey is not just about hoarding dimes and nickels. It's a daily reminder to put your finances first. To feed your monkey is to nourish your dreams and take your financial life by the *cojones.*

OFF TO THE RACES!

So here we have it: the accounts have been discussed, and your head has been properly scrubbed with a Brillo pad of self-examination in an effort to get down to the basics: what you have, what you want, and how you might get there. In other words, we've gathered the ingredients. Let's cook!

Our first stop is savings. Hoarding action figures and Cabbage Patch dolls in the hope that they will pay off big one day is not a plan. And real estate, if you do the math, is not as reliable in the long run as investing. So we are going to break this chapter down into three main sections, each dedicated to one of the three most important savings accounts in the lives of independent workers.

In order to take the next few steps, you will need the following:

- the financial information you gathered in chapters 2 and 3, including your earnings history, your fixed monthly costs, and your debt profile;
- access to your money-management software, if you use it;
- account(s) at an online bank. (You will create these over the course of this chapter.) If you have not chosen an online bank yet, do so now. You may look at the suggestions we put in the appendix or choose one of your own based on our recommendations or friends' recommendations (we think ours are best . . .);
- paper, pen, and calculator for any necessary calculations.

Once you have assembled these few goodies, you are ready to move on.

WHAT TO EXPECT

In this chapter, we are going to present the three key accounts that are most vital to the majority of freelancers and independent workers. These three accounts are your foundation in the Freelance Finance system and will serve as the core of your initial savings. You will build on these as you progress through the system, eventually creating new accounts dedicated to your other specific savings goals.

For each account, we will discuss the appropriate percentage to set aside and potential savings goals that you should keep in mind. Remember: people earn very differently and spend very differently. We will give you suggestions about how to tailor this information to your specific set of circumstances, but in order to really get the most out of this you will have to pay close attention and you will have to have completed the exercises in the first few chapters. You can't make a BLT without bacon, lettuce, and tomato, and you can't build wealth without information about your earnings, spending, and debt. So if you haven't done those exercises already, go back and do them now!

This chapter will help you . . .

- set up your accounts;
- decide what percentage you wish to pay into each.

You will then be prepared for when that next check comes in the door. Each time you're paid—no matter how big the check, no matter how small—you are going to deduct these percentages from the total amount of your check and place those designated amounts into completely separate accounts that are *not* accessible by ATM. These accounts will be dedicated to specific goals and purposes. No more mingling of funds!

THE HOLY TRINITY OF SAVINGS

And here they are. Allow us to present the three key accounts that virtually all freelancers and independent workers need. Coincidentally, they are the same accounts that very few of us bother to establish.

- the Emergency Account
- the Retirement Account
- the Tax Account

"Hey—hang on a minute," you might say. "Why did I do all that work in the first section, identifying my dreams, if none of them are even listed here? Where's my #@**!!! kayak?!"

First, we didn't say that these were the *only* accounts that you would be setting up. We are just saying that you need to take care of these accounts first. If you don't have these three bases covered, you are not going to be in a good position down the road to fulfill any of your dreams—kayak included. You will end up paying a price for not establishing these, whether that price is a nonexistent down payment for the house you've been eyeing that finally came on the market or mounting debt.

Habitually funding these three accounts can elevate your financial life to incredibly comfortable new heights. It will help put you in a position where you will not have to rely on your credit card to make ends meet when a client is late with payment. As the accounts grow, you will gain confidence and peace of mind knowing that you *can* make your business work. And it will make tax time a whole lot more predictable and a lot less stroke inducing.

Notice that two of these three accounts—taxes and retirement—speak directly to the kind of financial housekeeping that independent workers have to deal with that most salaried workers do not. These are essentially surrogate accounts that cover the kinds of costs that are normally covered by employers without employees' having to think about them. The third account, for emergencies, speaks to any working stiff on the planet with a pulse—everyone needs it. However, this account takes on much greater importance in the life of the freelancer because of our variable payments and the tricky timing that often accompanies them.

	EMERGENCY ACCOUNT	RETIREMENT ACCOUNT	TAX ACCOUNT
What it is	Money to get you out of tight financial spots	Money for when you're done working	Money for the Tax Man!
Who needs it	Everyone, salaried and independent workers alike	Anyone who doesn't want to live on cat food in their seventies	Anyone who earns untaxed income
Where it is held	Online bank*	Online bank*	Online bank*
Savings goal	At least six months' worth of living expenses (Some advisers now recommend a six- to twelve-month cushion.)	Enough money to live comfortably in your golden years (Amounts will vary wildly depending on your retirement lifestyle and when you want to hang up your working spurs.)	Enough money to pay your quarterly taxes and any additional annual taxes

*Remember: No ATM access!!!

Establishing these three accounts will go a long way toward shoring up your financial profile. Let's look at each one individually and assess the role it can play in your new approach to money management.

THE EMERGENCY ACCOUNT

Kathleen Campbell knows firsthand the importance of having an Emergency Account. When her highly paid husband lost his job as the vice president of a home-building corporation at the start of the Florida housing crash, their family supplemented Kathleen's self-employed pay with savings until her husband could find another job.

"Our money situation changed overnight," says Kathleen. "It took him ten months to find a job. During that whole time, we lived off what I brought home and what we had in savings. I'm proud to say that after that whole ordeal, we did not go into debt."

Of course, Kathleen knows a good deal about financial cushions. As founder of Campbell Financial Partners in Fort Myers, Florida, she's a self-employed financial planner who specializes in advising middle-class Americans on how to handle their money. "There's no way around it," she says, "an emergency fund is extremely important. You must have a bucket of money saved up that you can dip into if something happens."

Independent workers are more likely than employed people to have these kinds of financial emergencies. No matter who you are, what you do, or where you work, you need to have this money set aside. Whether or not you take a salary, whether or not your spouse has a great job, the Emergency Account is a must.

Emergency Accounts have wisely been touted for many years as a necessary part of any safe and sane financial profile. In the mainstream financial press—geared primarily to those with jobs—the account is presented as a way to protect yourself in the case of *unexpected financial disasters* or *interrupted income.* While all workers stand an equal chance of experiencing the first, independent workers are more likely than employed people to experience the second.

It can also be used for those unexpected and hefty bills that always manage to show up at precisely the wrong time (hello, car trouble), and it can help with unexpected—and uncovered—medical costs if you don't have a separate health savings account or another account set aside for medical bills. Everyone likes to think that freelancers don't really have "jobs," so it is a pleasant, if small, perk to know that we can't lose them. But things do happen that can prevent independent workers from working, whether it is illness or the disappearance of a client you've relied on for three years.

SETTING IT UP

Now go to your online bank and open your Emergency Account. If you'd like, give it a name that makes you smile, one that speaks to your goals or to the way you would like to feel when thinking about your finances. Whatever blows your skirt up. We like to call ours the "Sunny Day" account. Though it is technically our "emergency" or "rainy day" account, we felt that those names were just inviting financial crisis, so we opted for a cheerier moniker. But hey—if you want to stick with the tried and true, by all means . . .

How will you fund your Emergency Account? We started quite small. From each paycheck we received, we tucked just 3 percent into our Emergency Account. At the time, we were virtually homeless and were struggling for cash. Not being able to spend that 3 percent seemed onerous. But in time we found it wasn't. We soon realized that we weren't really missing it that much.

After just a few months, we switched to 5 percent. At first, the numbers didn't seem that impressive, but it didn't take long before we had a significant sum. We weren't up to six months' savings yet, but we knew that if we got a tad behind we had options other than the credit card or feigning a terminal illness for our mortgage company.

The experts are divided these days about how much money should be in the Emergency Account. The classic prescription has been three to six months. But if the worldwide economy tanks like the *Titanic*, you're going to wish you had socked away more than that. These days, a lot of financial advisers are telling their clients to shoot for six to twelve months. Others, like Kathleen, are hesitant to go that far. "It's fine if you have the money," she says, "but I don't want to tell a person who is living paycheck to paycheck that they need a year of income in their emergency fund, because they will just go home and save nothing."

In the end, obviously, the amount is up to you. The goal is to save a realistic amount that allows you to have some peace of mind.

Here are the basic rules governing the Emergency Account:

- Choose a percentage that you're comfortable with. Remember: you will also be setting aside money for retirement and taxes. Choose a percentage now, and if you need to come back and adjust after you read the next few sections, that's OK too.

- Dip in only if it's a real emergency—something that affects your ability to cover your fixed monthly costs.

- You *must* replenish the money you take out. You must put the money back. You have to replace the money. (Hmmm . . . are there any other ways we can say that?)

Since emergency money must be ready to use quickly, you can't really invest it in financial instruments such as stocks or bonds, which may fluctuate or need to be sold off in order to raise cash. Instead, in the short term, park emergency money in a *money-market account (MMA)* or a *savings account* at an online bank. In the long term, you might consider transferring your nest egg to a *money-market mutual fund* held at a brokerage. Some of these funds come equipped with their own checkbook, which leads people to think they are "just like a bank account." Well, not exactly. Though very safe, money-market mutual funds are not FDIC insured. But they often pay far better interest than what you're probably going to get at a brick-and-mortar bank. It's a toss-up whether they pay better than just keeping the money at your online bank. Compare rates before you leap.

HOW TO USE IT

Used correctly, the Emergency Account is a financial cushion that keeps you off credit cards and from raiding far more important money, such as your retirement or tax funds. For the self-employed, it may sometimes be a kind of slush fund. This can get hairy, but at the beginning of a career especially, getting used to the now-it's-here-now-it's-not cash flow can be nightmarish.

For example: stretch the confines of your mind and try to imagine a world in which a client doesn't pay on time, forgets to submit payment, forgets to file the contract with accounting, or . . .

"Would you mind resending the invoice?" the voice at the other end of the line asks sweetly.

Your mind reels. You did everything you were supposed to do. This isn't *fair.* Your evil twin is itching to respond, "How about before I do that, you take a second and get your head out of your [insert body part here] for five minutes and go find the invoice I sent you two months ago so I don't have to wait another forty-five days for payment? How does that sound?"

If only. You reply, "Certainly, I can get that over to you this afternoon." Now you know that by the time the second invoice gets processed, the payment will be late—and you will be late paying several bills, if you don't figure something out.

Enter the Emergency Account. You may need to dip into it to cover monthly expenses when your checks don't come monthly and you haven't been able to set money aside for your fixed monthly costs in your Overhead Account (see chapter 7). Do not use it because you just have to treat yourself to dinner but can't really afford it. That's not an emergency. That's life.

Here's the big question: what is an emergency? Take a peek at these three scenarios and decide if they qualify.

1. A client is paying late and you don't have the money for rent.

2. Your car broke down and you had to put the repairs on the credit card. Now you want to pay off that charge all at once.

3. You want to buy a new computer for work and don't have the cash on hand.

We would say that number one is an emergency for most of us, number two is debatable, and three is a no-no.

However—and this is the part that requires discipline—once the village idiot does manage to finally pay you for the work that you did *five* months ago now, you must not only replace the money that you took out of the Emergency Account but also contribute the established percentage that you would normally send to the Emergency Account from each check that comes in the door (unless, of course, simply replacing the money keeps you at your cushion goal).

Should you have to, here's how to dip into the Emergency Account.

STEP 1: IDENTIFY THE EMERGENCY The rent is due and you don't have the money in your Spending Account. You are owed several checks from vendors or clients, but none of them have yet arrived. You are certain you will get the money soon, just not in time to help you out of your bind. This is clearly a case of interrupted income and one that impacts your ability to cover your fixed monthly costs. It is an emergency.

STEP 2: MAKE THE FUNDS AVAILABLE Go ahead and transfer the funds from the online bank to your Spending Account at the brick-and-mortar bank.

STEP 3: WRITE YOURSELF AN IOU On a sheet of paper, write what you owe yourself and commit to paying it back. This might feel stupid or hokey, but this is exactly what you would be doing—albeit more formally—if you were to borrow money from yourself via an old 401(k) account or a home-equity line of credit.

STEP 4: ASSESS YOUR ABILITY TO REPAY—THEN DO IT As your clients pay you, send the established percentages from each of these checks to their respective accounts. See what money's left over and make sure you can cover your upcoming fixed costs. Once these are covered, pay what you can to extinguish your IOU. Do this as many times as necessary until the money is paid back. Celebrate with a (cheap) meal or drink. Yay. You're a successful microlender!

Paying yourself back and making your regular investment can be quite a blow to your paycheck, so you will probably want to pay yourself back slowly. Either way, knowing that there is some money set aside for the tight times—and for many freelancers, those times come all too often—is so calming. It allows you to focus on work, not be paralyzed by the fear following a mad dash to the mailbox only to find a grocery circular, some car-wash coupons, and, if you're really lucky, more bills.

Once you've begun to establish your Emergency Account, you can use your need to dip into it as a kind of gauge for how your work life is going and whether or not your earning matches your overhead and spending habits. Combined with the information you gathered in chapters 2 and 3, the need for and use of the Emergency Account will help you clarify what's working and what's not.

THE RETIREMENT ACCOUNT

Independent workers are the gunslingers of the work world. The successful ones take pride in the fact that they have made their own way in life. But even crusty old cowpokes realize there's a time to hang up one's six-guns. How well do they fare then?

Frankly, not so well. Most Americans—freelancers or not—do a terrible job of saving for the future. Scratch that. Most people do a lousy job of saving, period. They assume that the future will simply be a continuation of the present. But that just isn't true. Despite the multivitamins you swallow, the carbs you shun, or the reps you crank out at the gym, someday you will probably get too old to work. And you won't see any more checks except the canceled ones you wrote yourself lying at the bottom of your desk drawer.

If that disturbs you, then think of it in a more positive light: wouldn't you love to retire early and devote the rest of your days to what matters most to you? Many people cling to the fantasy of retiring at forty or fifty, but they don't understand what that really means. *I'll just make a pile of money and live off that,* they tell themselves. But how does that work exactly?

True financial independence means you've reached a point where the money you're earning from your investments exceeds your current or foreseeable expenses. Your money does the work, so you don't have to. The trick is socking away enough money and investing it intelligently to reach this point.

Why don't many people achieve this goal? They make lots of mistakes. They wait too long to start saving. They save inconsistently: a lot this year, too little the next. Or they are stuck in a pattern of denial: *Why do I need to save for retirement? I'm only [insert age here]. I have time to save.*

Independent workers are the worst when it comes to this. The gunslinger attitude has trained them to think they can roll with the punches forever. One of our friends, whom you'll meet later, hasn't started a retirement fund, despite annual entreaties from his accountant to stick some cash in an IRA. How does this forty-four-year-old shrug it off? "I'll get by," he says, epitomizing the attitude of many freelancers. "I'll figure something out. I always have."

But the truth is, none of us can afford to wait. Everyone wants to be a millionaire, but few recognize that they can achieve this quite effortlessly simply by saving. The youngest reader of this book—a twentysomething temp—*really* has a shot at building the most wealth of all. Why? Because the younger you are when you start saving, the richer you'll be. The miracle of compound interest is no joke.

Imagine that you earn forty thousand dollars a year. Say you managed to save 15 percent of your income every year until you retire at age seventy. (We'll assume an average of 8 percent return on your investment.) Look at the difference in wealth between the twentysomething who started saving early and the freelancers who waited until they got slapped upside the head by their accountants.

AGE NOW	MONEY INVESTED PER YEAR	NUMBER OF YEARS SAVING	ACTUAL DOLLARS INVESTED	AMOUNT AT AGE 70
25	$6,000	45	$270,000	$2.4 million
35	$6,000	35	$210,000	$1.07 million
45	$6,000	25	$150,000	$454,718

Source: Created using Hugh Chou's Simple Savings Calculator (www.hughchou.org/calc/savings.cgi)

Look at those numbers. Astounding, eh? The more you save, the more your money grows. And the younger you start saving, the more money you have.

Now, you can pick apart the data all you like. You can say things like "Well, I don't earn forty thousand dollars a year" or "Nobody's salary is that stable—or that fixed" or "You'll never earn eight percent interest in this economy."

You're right, of course. Everyone's situation is different. And that's why, if you're not convinced, you need to run your own numbers through various online calculators to see how a program of persistent saving would transform your life.

If you already have one or more retirement funds and are diligently saving, congratulations. If you're an independent worker whose spouse has a retirement account at work, you're certainly better off. But the two of you probably need to sit down and figure out how your freelance earnings can augment what your spouse is already saving through his or her employer. And if you're an unmarried or underfunded freelancer, this is your chance to become familiar with some of the products designed to help the self-employed save.

Earlier, we said you needed a retirement account in the bank, and we firmly believe this. But your bank account is not the final destination for this money. Bank accounts are safe, but they don't offer the kind of long-term interest you'll need to earn the big bucks. At a certain point, you must transfer this money from your online bank to a dedicated retirement account. This account can contain various investments, such as mutual funds, stocks, or bonds.

Yes, we know the stock market has tanked spectacularly on occasion, but you still need to be there. It's one of the single best ways to earn money. Look at what that twenty-five-year-old earned on a $270,000 investment in forty-five years: $2.4 million. You don't get there by swapping comic books.

Employed people have their 401(k)s, but self-employed people have an impressive arsenal of savings instruments as well. In fact, some experts—such as Jeff Kostis of JK Financial Planning in Vernon Hills, Illinois—point out that self-employed individuals can potentially sock away more money than employed people. "It's always a struggle to get a business going," says Jeff, "but once you start being successful, there's a lot to be said for being self-employed." That's because some of the retirement plans available to self-employed people actually have higher maximum annual contributions than the $16,500 max 401(k) contribution (in 2010) enjoyed by your employed happy-hour buddies.

So why aren't more independent workers rolling in cash? Because they don't take advantage of these generous opportunities.

We're going to discuss each of these savings vehicles briefly, but bear in mind that they are not created equal. Some accounts are best established by self-employed people with employees. Other accounts are so laborious to establish that you wouldn't want to go there unless you had a very high income. And we'd like to remind you that only you—acting on the advice of a financial professional, accountant, or certified financial planner—can choose the best combination of accounts for your individual situation.

IRAS, SEPS, AND OTHER IMPORTANT ACRONYMS

Self-employed individuals can take advantage of one or more of the following types of accounts.

SIMPLIFIED EMPLOYEE PENSION INDIVIDUAL RETIREMENT ACCOUNT (SEP-IRA): These accounts are popular with freelancers for a reason: they're so easy to open that you can do it online in a few minutes. Each year, you have until April 15 to deposit up to 20 percent of your previous year's *net self-employment income*—your income after deductions—up to a 2010 maximum of . . . wait for it . . . forty-nine thousand dollars. *In-freaking-credible, right?* (If you're an employee of your own corporation, you can sock away 25 percent of your salary.) SEP contributions are tax deductible: that means taxes are deferred on that money until you retire, when your tax rate is likely to be less. Say you earn fifteen thousand dollars in income after deductions. If you put three thousand dollars in a SEP, right off the bat, without making any other genius financial moves, your taxable income drops to twelve thousand dollars. Three thousand bucks are off the table. This is a gift from Uncle Sam, and not nearly enough independent workers avail themselves of it. There's one catch: the minute you hire an employee, you must contribute the same amount of money to that employee's SEP as you're paying into your own. "A SEP is great if you have no employees or your only employees are relatives," says Jeff the financial planner. "It helps you build wealth within your family unit."

SIMPLE IRA: We wanted to ignore this account, but our editor was getting all completist on us. These accounts are for self-employed people who have no more than one hundred employees. During the year, you, the boss, would divert a portion of your paycheck to your Simple IRA. You would also divert a portion of each employee's paycheck to his or her Simple IRA, and at year's end, you would match up to 3 percent of the employee's contributions with company money. In the end, though, neither you nor your employees can sock away more than $11,500 a year, or $14,000 for employees over the age of fifty. (These maximums are quite low compared to those of the other retirement plans we're telling you about.) Last, any cash you put in for your employees is theirs to keep, even if they decide to quit the day after becoming recipients of your largesse. The Simple IRA is indeed a simple way to build a 401(k)-like plan for your small business. We just happen to think you can do *way* better.

SOLO 401(K): Also called Individual 401(k)s, these accounts are astoundingly generous if you have the cash and patience. They allow you to save 100 percent of the first $16,500 of the salary you're earning from your small business or self-employed income after deductions. On top of that, you can save an additional 25 percent of your salary, or 20 percent of your self-employed income after deductions. All contributions are tax deductible. Dollar for dollar, the Solo 401(k) lets you shelter more of your money than any of the other plans we've discussed thus far. The catch: the paperwork is slightly more complicated, not many financial services companies offer them, and plans can cost up to $250 in annual maintenance fees. The plans are really designed for businesses whose owners are the only employees. The minute you hire an employee—even your kid—the Solo 401(k) is no longer solo and you must expand your plan to offer your employees the same benefits you're enjoying.

KEOGH ACCOUNTS: If your business is doing extremely well, you might consider a Keogh plan, which closely mimics the types of benefits you might find at a conventional corporation. These plans come in different types. A profit-sharing plan, for instance, permits small business owners to sock away as much as $49,000 per person annually for themselves and their employees. A defined-benefits plan, on the other hand, will let you go as high as $195,000 a year in contributions, but they're for business owners who don't have employees. The catch in both plans is that you will need to hire a financial services company to manage the whole thing, submit annual reports, and hit target contributions determined by an actuary. This sounds like a pain in the bum, but some high-earning independent workers see no other way to save tax free. By the way, it's not necessary to have employees to take advantage of these plans, so if you've got the dough, go Keogh.

But wait. That's not all!

ROTH IRA: Want more? The Roth is the cherry on top of all these other accounts. Even if you've already squirreled away cash in any of the above accounts, you are still eligible to place five thousand dollars a year (ten thousand dollars for married couples) into a Roth account. You will need to pay taxes on the money you put in there, but the income earned is tax free. You can take it out when you retire and not pay a single cent of tax on what you've earned.

TAXABLE BROKERAGE ACCOUNTS: Retirement accounts are designed to help you save in some "tax-advantaged" way. But just because you've maxed out all your retirement accounts for the year doesn't mean you can't save any more. You can still save as much as you want or can afford in a brokerage account that will allow you to buy mutual funds, stocks, and bonds, just as you would in a retirement account. Be aware, of course, that each year any income you earn in this account will be taxed at your current rate.

WHAT ABOUT LITTLE OLD ME?

With all these accounts to choose from, what's a small freelancer to do? We knew you would try to get us to make financial recommendations, even though our lawyer said we shouldn't. But OK, here goes. Assuming you accept our disclaimer that you should check with an accountant or financial planner about your specific situation, we will say that most independent workers who run a single-person business should probably have three accounts for their retirement savings:

1. **A SEP-IRA:** Dirt cheap to run and easy to open, this account will allow you to reduce the amount of money you need to pay each year for your taxes. (Max contribution:

20 percent of your net self-employed income, aka profit, up to forty-nine thousand dollars in 2010.)

2. **A ROTH IRA:** Equally simple to operate, this account will allow you to sock away still more cash. You pay taxes on any contributions you make now, but money continues to grow tax free, and you won't owe a dime when you retire. (Max contribution: five thousand dollars as of 2010.)

3. **A TAXABLE BROKERAGE ACCOUNT:** Yet another way to save—albeit in a taxable way. Requires just a bit more effort to keep track of year-end statements for tax purposes. (Max contribution: whatever you like!)

If you choose to go this route, you will open all three of these accounts at a financial services company like the ones we list in our appendix. Some of them require a minimum amount to open an account. While some have minimums as low as fifty dollars, others—such as Vanguard, one of the better-known and more respected names in the business—require a three-thousand-dollar minimum deposit to open many of their accounts. If you don't have that much money in your retirement bank account, wait until you do. Then open the new account. After that initial contribution, most firms will let you send as little as fifty to a hundred dollars at a time. In some cases, firms will waive the required contribution if you are opening a retirement account and are willing to set up an automatic deposit of, say, fifty to a hundred dollars monthly.

SETTING UP AND USING THE RETIREMENT ACCOUNT

Open your Retirement Account at your trusty online bank.

As with your Emergency Account, you may be starting quite small. The important thing is to start and to stick with it. We swear, you will be raising your percentages in no time. The Retirement Account is a holding cell for your retirement savings. Ultimately, the money will be transferred into one or more of the accounts already described in this chapter. This is usually done on a quarterly basis, when you check in with your accountant or tax guru regarding your quarterly taxes. (More on these darling folks later.)

Here are the basic rules governing the Retirement Account:

- Choose a percentage that you're comfortable with. Somewhere between 10 percent and 15 percent would be wonderful. Twenty percent is a stupendous amount to save for your retirement. But we understand if you're reluctant to start that high. The important thing is to pick a figure and start saving that percentage in the bank account you have established to hold this money until you're ready to invest it. Remember: you can always adjust the percentage up or down later.
- The entire percentage you save will stay in your online account until it is invested in one of the vehicles mentioned here.
- Check in with your financial guide on a quarterly basis. Depending on what you've earned in a particular quarter, he or she will advise you how much you can safely contribute to the accounts you've chosen to establish. (How much you can contribute to your SEP, for example, is based on what you make, whereas the maximum contributions for the Roth or other investment instruments in your growing portfolio are not.) If you've been a good little saver, you'll have that money.

If you have chosen to establish three accounts—a SEP, a Roth, and a taxable brokerage account—the order in which you invest in these could be as follows.

Say you've been setting aside 10 percent of your gross earnings in your Retirement Account. At the end of the first quarter of the year, you look at your online bank and you have $1,500.

1. You speak with your accountant, who informs you that, based on your year-to-date earnings and anticipated deductions, you can safely invest four hundred dollars for now in your SEP.
2. You transfer the four hundred dollars to your SEP account.
3. The other $1,200 can either be . . .
    a. invested in your Roth, if you have not yet reached the maximum contribution;
    b. invested in a taxable brokerage account; or
    c. left alone in your interest-earning Retirement Account at the online bank until the end of the fiscal year, when all the financial chickens come home to roost. That way, if you're short on taxes or find out you can contribute more to your SEP than initially estimated, the money is there.

When your Roth is fully funded and your tax guru says you can't contribute any more to your SEP, any additional savings can go into a taxable brokerage account or other investment vehicle mentioned here.

REMEMBER TO INVEST

Merely making contributions to your SEP or Roth doesn't necessarily mean you have invested the money. Typically, these accounts merely hold the money in a money-market mutual fund until you specifically instruct the company to buy bonds or shares of stocks and mutual funds for you. Money-market funds are safe investments, but they often don't pay much more interest than the online bank account you just transferred your money from. To really invest for the future, you must seek a better return on your money. Better rewards mean accepting higher risk. If you invest in mutual funds, you'll be spreading that risk among lots of companies. We don't want to get bogged down in tips on how to play the market. We'd rather you commit first to saving money, then to educating yourself about stock-market investments. But we'll give you a few tips to get you started.

Ideally, you will adopt the buy-and-hold strategy advised by most sensible financial planners. You'll buy a mutual fund or stock and hold it—ignoring market ups and downs—and sell in your golden years when it has risen considerably in value. The kinds of investments we recommend—index funds and target-date funds—are an easy way to get your foot in the door.

- *Target-date funds* are a mix of funds weighted by percentage to your specific date of retirement, such as 2045, 2055, or 2065. When you're young and can withstand more volatile shocks to your portfolio, these funds may consist of 80 percent stocks and 20 percent bonds. (In general, stocks are riskier.) As you get older, reflecting your diminishing ability to accept risk, these funds automatically dial down the stock percentage to a more conservative mix. However, some of these funds are way too conservative for our taste. We think people should choose dates that are ten or fifteen years *later* than they intend to retire.

- *Index funds* are low-cost mutual funds that mimic the results of a particular stock index, such as the Standard & Poor's 500 or the Dow Jones Industrial Average. You'll pay less than half a percent of your earnings a year to the firms that manage these funds. By contrast, a flashy stock fund that's actively managed by a "name" manager might cost you 2 percent of your profits.

Target-date and index funds aren't terribly sexy. You won't be phoning your broker at the market's opening each day and screaming for him or her to "Buy six thousand shares!" or "Sell! Sell! Sell!" People who make the market sound complicated, exciting, or absolutely in need of constant intervention are usually those who have a stake in your buying and selling. Guess who those people are? Stockbrokers and their employers. They are day-to-day traders and are highly vulnerable to short-term market swings. They also make tons of money on transaction fees. You don't have to play that game to build your wealth.

This doesn't mean that you shouldn't dump a mutual fund that turns out to be a dog. It *does* mean you should think carefully before you invest. Read up. (We give you educational sources in the appendix.) Pick a strategy and stick with it. You should not be ashamed to choose investments that cost you as little as possible to maintain. We were cheered recently to hear the advice Warren Buffett, the legendary investor and billionaire, gave a young man who asked what he should do with his first million. "Invest it in an index fund—and get back to work," quipped the sage of Omaha.

If low-cost investments are A-OK according to a billionaire, then they're OK for you and for us. The slow-and-steady approach to wealth is a fine way to get started with your retirement fund.

OUR FINANCIAL PLANNER WISH LIST

Financial planners like Kathleen and Jeff are like money coaches. They sit down with your financial playing field spread out in front of them, crunch the numbers, and come up with all the winning plays you need to execute to get your money on track. Here's what to keep in mind when hiring a financial planner:

- Hire a planner who works for fees paid by clients only. Avoid anyone who makes their money off commissions from various investment products they sell you. They may advertise their services as "free," but it's hard to trust the advice they're giving you if they're getting what amounts to a kickback.
- Choose a planner who is a fiduciary. This means that they are required to put your needs before their own. They should be willing to put this in writing.
- Choose a planner affiliated with either the National Association of Personal Financial Advisors (NAPFA) or the Garrett Planning Network. Some planners belong to both organizations.
- Realize that spending some money now will pay off later. Hourly rates for planners range from $120 an hour to $400

an hour. This might sound like a lot, but it's the best money you'll ever spend.

- Tailor your planning to your specific needs. Many planners offer packages geared to analyzing various facets of your money life. For example, if you were just engaged to be married and haven't done a financial checkup with your bride-to-be, you could go to a planner and do a financial checkup that looks at how you two can merge your finances. You might be offered a retirement checkup or tuition planning checkup.

THE TAX ACCOUNT

When Joe first went freelance, he sought the advice of a friend who had been in the self-employed trenches for quite some time. Her approach to saving for taxes was simple: as each check came in, she socked away a third (roughly 30 percent) into a separate account intended for taxes alone. Then each quarter, when she needed to pay her estimated taxes, she dipped into the fund. At the end of the year, after she paid the big, bad final payment to the Tax Man on April 15, any money that remained in the account she paid into her savings. While this approach doesn't provide for the kind of dedicated savings needed to cover all your bases, it did teach Joe a few things. He gave it a try.

He diligently took one-third of each check and socked it away in a separate account, vowing not to touch it until tax time. Unfortunately, he wasn't disciplined enough elsewhere. He never got around to paying estimated taxes; he just slacked off until April 15. And because he took the well-intentioned advice of a friend rather than consulting a professional, he didn't save any other money for himself. The first year there was more than enough money set aside for state and federal taxes and the accountant, to boot. Joe felt oddly rich, in a way, almost as though he had somehow saved *too* much money.

So then—SPLAT!!—he fell off the wagon. He stopped saving, assuming he could just pay out of pocket, since he thought he'd "oversaved" in the past. One brutal year he got hit with a five-thousand-dollar tax bill and—surprise, surprise—didn't have the money. It went on a low-interest credit card instead, and the vicious cycle of debt continued. It would be years before he would begin working on a plan to save not only for his taxes, but for retirement and emergencies as well.

Joe never forgot the wallet-skewering pain of that five-thousand-dollar bill. And if you count the interest he had to pay on top of the original bill because he had to slap it on a credit card, the cost was considerably more. Ouch.

Years later, Joe had changed his ways. He had begun saving for taxes and everything else and diligently paid his estimated taxes each quarter. He shared his burgeoning technique for designated saving with a fellow independent worker. She promptly proclaimed him completely and utterly nuts. Her idea of saving was to take a hundred dollars from every check that came in. She never had enough to pay her taxes. In fact, she never had enough money to pay for anything. She insisted that she couldn't spare 15 percent for taxes every year. She swore up and down that there was no way she could come up with another 10 percent for savings and retirement. She was a freelancer, after all. She wasn't made of money.

And yet when she was employed, she had routinely had

33 percent of her gross pay lopped from her earnings every freaking week and hadn't thought twice about it. If you're going to be self-employed, you must pounce as ruthlessly on your paychecks as the government does. Trust us—they're not skimping on the tax percentage. So you have to do the same. It's the only way you can survive over the long term and the only way you'll be able to foster the prosperity you deserve.

SETTING IT UP

Open a Tax Account at your online bank. Give it an appropriate nickname, perhaps something mildly profane, if that helps you channel your anger about paying out your hard-earned dough to The Man. Once that's done, it is time to decide just how much you need to set aside for your taxes out of each check.

There are two main ways to figure this out:

- Ask a professional.
- Do the math.

ASK A PROFESSIONAL

We suggest getting help. (See "Reaching Out for Help" on page 152.) We asked our tax man, based on our most recent returns, to tell us how much we needed to set aside in order to cover our taxes. Based on past earnings and taxation, combined with projected income, he gave us a ballpark number. But that's just the beginning.

Asking your guru what you should set aside based on past experience is not enough. What we make year to year changes, so while that initial estimate provides guidance from January through March, we have quarterly conversations with our tax man about how much we've earned and how much we think will come in the door down the line. If necessary, we can adjust what we set aside that year as we move forward.

So sit down with your new best friend and ask him or her: On average, what percentage of my annual income is going to pay for all of my taxes? Specifically, what am I paying for city, state, and federal taxes, and your fee on top of it? He or she should be able to give you an average percentage based on your last three years of tax returns.

DO THE MATH

Yes, math again. Serves you right for not finding someone to help you with your taxes. If you do not have a tax man—or woman—who can advise you on such things, here's a good way to get started. Take those tax returns that you gathered in chapter 2. Focus on the more recent returns, say the last three years.

1. Look at how much you made—gross—each of those three years. Come up with an average. Then figure out how much you paid in taxes—to city, state, and federal governments—and convert this to an average, too.

2. Now you've got two numbers: the average income for those three years and the average amount of taxes you've been paying. Now you can figure out the average tax rate that you've paid. The math would look like this:

$$\frac{\text{total tax paid}}{\text{amount earned}} \times 100 = \text{tax rate paid (percent)}$$

3. Whatever the final number is—10, 15, 20 percent, or whatever—you will now have a ballpark figure on which

> to base your saving. Bear in mind that this figure is still an average. If your income or deductions fluctuated greatly in the last three years, you might need to revise your percentage up or down. If you discover that you have paid an average of 11 percent in taxes for the last three years, why not round that up to 12 percent or 15 percent? The great thing about doing this is that if you don't end up needing it for your taxes, you've still got some extra cash saved up.

If you have *never* set aside money for your taxes during the year and are embarking on paying your quarterly taxes for the first time ever (good for you!), then start with a percentage that is reasonable for the income you expect to earn in your business. If you file a Schedule C, which many freelancers do, you are taxed on your profit—not your gross income—whatever is left over after you've accounted for all your deductions. However, also remember that you can't spend your life claiming a loss on your business without showing that you're trying to make it work. If you can't make a profit, you have to demonstrate a profit *motive.* This is the government's way of saying they want you to really really try your darnedest to make a profit (three out of five consecutive years) so that they can get their hands on some of it. Otherwise, years of no profit whatsoever and they will consider what you do a hobby, which means that you cannot deduct any delicious expenses. This presents yet one more reason to be dealing with a seasoned tax professional, one who makes him- or herself available throughout the year in case you need to ask about things like profit motive. (See the appendix for more on profit motive from the IRS.)

Say you're just starting out and set aside 10 percent for taxes in year 1. You'll either be fine or later discover you should have saved more. Hopefully, it's not such a huge bump that you can't shell out the difference at the end of the year out of savings. Based on what you've now learned, adjust your percentage depending on what your expert tells you, what you've just earned, and what you project to make in the coming year.

REACHING OUT FOR HELP

If you don't have a tax preparer or an accountant and you still do your own taxes each year, then you have a fool for a client. You *must* enlist professional help with this so you don't have to worry about anything other than being as successful and focused on your career and your life as you can be. Trust us: the best thing you can do is get yourself a good, quality tax preparer and then shamelessly rely on that person throughout the year—not just at tax time.

Stu Minikes, a tax preparer working in both New Jersey and New York City, was telling us once about the tax challenges faced by the independent worker. (Like we needed an accountant to tell us!) "The biggest mistake that self-employed people make is not listening to me when I tell them to pay their estimated taxes," he explained. "And then they wind up owing a lot of money at the end of the year."

And then there's the record keeping. What do you think the IRS is going to do, simply *trust* that you spent $573 on express postage and $1,794 on business-related travel? "Keep track of your expenses and keep good records," Minikes advises. "Just give us the summary of your expenses, but keep the receipts, because if you ever get audited, you have to be able to back everything up. Some people don't, and then you can get into a really big jam."

His advice for his self-employed clients is simple: "They give me a call on a quarterly basis and tell me their approximate income. . . . I don't have a crystal ball, but I come up with a ballpark figure. That's why it's called an estimate."

Minikes agrees that it's in the best interest of anyone who is self-employed to hire a good tax preparer. "There are a lot of things to know about deductions, about paying estimated taxes. Some people don't realize the consequences."

One freelancer we talked to—a young hairstylist named Kate—admitted that sorting out her finances was the biggest challenge when she went freelance. After years of waitressing, then going to school to learn to cut hair, she was finally ready to rent a chair at a salon and set up shop. Very quickly, she noticed that there was a big difference between the freelance stylists and the ones who worked directly for the salon. The staffers never had to set aside money to pay rent on their chairs, buy supplies, buy health insurance, and pay their taxes.

"My very first year I didn't pay very much in estimated taxes," says the twenty-eight-year-old, "so it kind of bit me in the ass at the end of the year."

For Kate, getting a dependable accountant has made all the difference. "Every year I'm getting a little better at figuring out what I need to bring to him," she says. "He helps me out immensely. There is so much that I don't know about. Nothing about my taxes is cut-and-dry. He knows the system much better than I do. We'll get together once a year and go over what I need to pay. The very first time we got together, he laid out everything I needed to do in the course of the year."

What should you look for in a tax preparer?

OUR TAX PREPARER WISH LIST

1. Someone who, duh, knows taxes. You don't necessarily need an accountant (although depending on your busi-

ness, you may), and accountants can be more expensive. What you do need is someone who specializes in taxes and who works with a number of self-employed clients. Be sure to ask.

2. Someone who charges a reasonable yearly fee, depending on the complexity of your return. If you work alone, are struggling to make a profit, and have a pretty manageable return, you shouldn't be paying the same rate as someone who has ten employees and a net profit of $250,000.

3. You absolutely, positively want someone you can contact throughout the year to ask about quarterly tax payments and retirement investments. This is key. At the end of each quarter, you should be able to send an e-mail to your tax preparer telling her how much money you've earned in that quarter and asking her to calculate your estimated taxes. You should also ask her to send you the vouchers you'll need to mail in your various payments. It's her job to do this for you. If she is unwilling to do this, wants too much money to perform this task, or is too distracted with other things to get back to you, get another tax professional. You deserve someone who takes your business seriously.

TO DEDUCT OR NOT TO DEDUCT

One of the other top reasons to get yourself a quality tax preparer or accountant is their ability to maneuver and manage your deductions. If you have tax-o-phobia and are one of those people who can barely stand to think about your taxes until sometime after April 10, focusing on the potential power of your deductions can help cure you and also whip you into shape on other fronts as well, inspiring you to be better about tracking your expenses and saving your receipts. (Have you gotten the financial software yet? Have you?) The tax code really is designed to help the self-employed person, and we are better off than the average employee because we can take deductions for things that salaried employees can't.

So what is deductible?

On the subject of deductible business expenses, the IRS has this to say:

To be deductible, a business expense must be both ordinary and necessary. An ordinary expense is one that is common and accepted in your trade or business. A necessary expense is one that is helpful and appropriate for your trade or business. An expense does not have to be indispensable to be considered necessary.

While the kinds of deductions you can take vary according to your job, a few classic examples of deductions available to independent workers include

- health insurance;
- office space (either separately or, if it's a home office, as a percentage of your home);
- computers and phones;
- office furniture;
- work-related travel;
- marketing and promotional materials;
- uniforms;
- tools and other equipment.

Most seasoned self-employed folks know about these, but there are those deductions that are less obvious, such as moving expenses, travel expenses if you have to go to another part of the country to seek specialized medical treatment, professional publications, and more. Kate, the hairstylist, was delighted to discover that she could deduct the cost of the professional scissors she uses to cut hair, not to mention all her other supplies. Musicians like our friend Dave, whom you'll meet momentarily, can deduct lots of wonderful stuff, such as guitars and sound equipment. The important thing to remember is that each and every profession is different, so be sure to ask your tax guru about specific deductions.

TIME TO PAY UP

Estimated taxes are due in April, June, September, and January. So at the end of each quarter (March 30, May 30, August 31, and December 31) tally what you've earned. E-mail your tax preparer at each of these intervals, tell her what you've earned thus far, find out what you should pay and how much you can set aside for investments such as your SEP.

To prep for your annual tax payment, start collecting all the tax-related statements, such as 1099s, that start trickling in by mail around January, and keep them safe in a folder for your accountant to look over as part of your year-end meeting. Another bonus of having dedicated savings for both retirement and taxes is that they can work together. Investing in some plans, such as the SEP, effectively reduces your taxable income. The more you save, the more you . . . save!

FREQUENTLY WHINED QUESTIONS (OR, DO YOU HAVE WHAT IT TAKES?)

We can hear you already: *Oh, my God! How can I do all this? 10 percent for this, 5 percent for that, another 15 percent here . . . I don't have that kind of money!* Think of it this way: If you save 25 percent of each check, you're keeping 75 percent. Doesn't that sound like a lot? If you were working for an employer, they would take *at least* that much. This also helps you clarify what you really need to earn and whether or not your overhead needs to be adjusted. How can you honestly examine overhead if you aren't paying for everything that needs to be covered? If you don't pay it now, you will pay for it—in taxes, increased debt, and ulcers—down the line.

One question that came up a lot for us as we were first thinking about putting this system to paper was: Will people really be disciplined enough to save money this way? The question is rooted in the notion that people are by nature bad savers, that they will routinely spend their cash on a quick thrill today, rather than delay that spending for a future goal. This belief is used to support the use of scheduled electronic withdrawals to set up weekly, biweekly, or monthly deposits, to ensure that you will save. This is by far the best possible route to take *if you have a salary.*

But we don't.

Our system, as you may have noticed, is strongly "analog." As each check comes in the door, you yourself must manually divvy up the cash—20 percent to retirement, 10 percent to your emergency fund, and so on—down the list to every account you've created. We believe that many independent workers would end up staring at a bunch of overdraft fees at the end of the month, not money in the bank, if they set up automatic withdrawals. That's just the way it is. Independent workers have a huge problem with cash flow. One month up, one month down. You often cannot predict or guarantee that on the third Friday of the month you will have the $150 that you intended to send to your retirement account.

Instead, our system is based on the way people saved money in the days before computers: by sheer, gut-wrenching will.

This is nothing new. "Back in the day," when they got their pay, say, every Friday, lots of folks would plop down at the kitchen table and divide the cash into various piles. This much for rent, that much for food, a little here for the future, and so on. If they could do that then, why can't we do it now? We can. When it's explained this way, people "get it"—they understand this low-tech approach, even if they somehow still crave the high-tech toys that theoretically absolve them of the need to apply discipline to their lives.

If you have worked freelance for a couple of years and have met with success, you already have enough discipline to save money this way. It takes discipline to work alone, to court customers and clients, to buckle down, do a job, and keep billing. So don't worry about being able to follow the system. You've got what it takes. Just start doing it.

We firmly believe that all of us have this kind of determination in our bones. We may not know it just yet, because we haven't seen it in a while. Fifty bucks flies out of our wallets for beer and wings on a Friday night without a second thought. But if we want something badly enough, we can summon the will from the depths of our wing-sated bellies.

WRAPPING IT ALL UP

If you do all of this regularly, you will always have enough to pay your taxes and you'll reap a few bucks here and there from the interest you're earning while that money is sitting in your accounts. If you stay disciplined, the system should work like clockwork. At first, you may be tempted to raid your Tax Account to pay other bills, or to take scuba lessons. Resist. As your Emergency Account grows, you'll always have *that* financial cushion to fall back on if you really need to, without ever touching your Tax Account or—God forbid—the retirement.

So let's talk percentages. As we've worked through this chapter, we've discussed choosing percentages for each of your Holy Trinity accounts. We've instructed you to start small, so that you stick with it. Many of you may be able to start with larger numbers, though, and you would be wise to do so. We will go into more detail about how these percentages work together in chapter 8, "Putting It All Together." In the meantime, remember: you can always adjust your percentages later if you need to.

So where do *you* start?

We would love it if you could start setting aside a minimum of 10 percent for your retirement; 15 percent would be better; 20 percent would be fantastic. If you've never saved like this before, you may want to start with 5 percent.

For taxes, you should talk with a pro and assess your individual situation. Again, we suggest doing the math and calculating the percentage tax you have paid in the past. Set that amount aside with each check or cash earnings that come in. If you have never, ever paid your estimated taxes, are new to freelancing, or routinely wait to be sucker punched by the government in April, then start by setting aside at least 15 percent. Is this enough? Maybe not. But it's a whole lot better than you've been doing, and you will gradually increase your amount from here. If you have been paying your taxes, but just not saving ahead for them, aim to set aside between 20 percent and 30 percent. You may owe more; you may have a refund coming. The point is, do yourself a favor and save for it. You can always adjust later based on careful analysis of your situation.

As for emergencies: If you have no cushion whatsoever, start by saving around 5 percent for emergencies. If you already have six months' worth of living expenses set aside, pat yourself on the back and put a little extra toward your retirement.

So yes, we know. That's 30 percent or more of your hard-earned buckaroos. But guess what? If you were working at an office, that's the very least that would be yanked out of your paycheck. And if you're still wondering about why we asked you to do all that work in chapter 2, tallying how much you really earn and how much you really spend, now you know. That information holds the key to the kind of percentages you can safely afford to set aside and still cover your fixed monthly costs.

So let's take a look at the percentages you've been considering throughout this chapter. Enter them here:

Emergency Account __________ percent

Retirement Account __________ percent

Tax Account ________________ percent

Total ____________________ percent

Look at that final number. Don't be scared. It won't bite you. This is a starting point. This is the number that represents a brand-new way of taking hold of your finances. If you are saying, *There is no way I can do this . . .*, then we suggest the following.

Look again at what you have earned on average over the last several years and what you've paid in taxes. What percentage have you been paying in taxes? Is the number listed here more or less? You paid it, right?

So you *can* do that—you already have been.

Now look at what you've spent over the last several years and what you owe, if anything, on credit cards. Look at the individual items. Can you honestly say that there is no room for saving?

If you have absolutely no questionable expenditures whatsoever, you are spending exactly what you earn on your bare necessities and nothing else, and you never buy food out, new clothes, etc., then maybe you have a leg to stand on. And if that really, truly, abso-positively is the case, you may want to think about ways in which you can lower your fixed monthly costs. But seriously, for most of us, the truth is that we haven't been managing our money in the best possible way. So the only real, sensible choice you have is to start paying yourself first. And start doing it *now.*

You *can* do this.

You *must* do this.

You *owe* it to yourself to do this.

You *deserve* this.

WHAT TO DO

Now you've begun to establish the accounts that you will rely on from today until . . . well, until. Before moving on to the next chapter, make sure you've done the following:

- Establish the three following accounts at an online bank: one each for emergency, retirement, and taxes. (pp. 126, 141, 147)

- Choose a percentage that you want to dedicate to each. Write down each percentage in the tally presented at the end of this chapter. (p. 160)

- Start to investigate the kinds of investment products you can buy with the money you are saving in your retirement fund. (p. 144)

CHAPTER 7

THE SPENDING ACCOUNT AS A FUNNEL FOR SAVINGS

Our musician friend Dave was one of the lucky ones: he graduated college with just a smidgen of debt because his parents footed the bill for much of his education. Now he was out on his own, living in the big city, playing his music, and temping at law firms to pay the bills. One day, a credit-card offer showed up in the mail. It seemed like a godsend to Dave, who filled out the form and was soon the proud owner of his own beautiful piece of plastic with a modest credit limit. "It wasn't much," he recalls. "Maybe five thousand dollars? I didn't care. I went on a spending spree and bought a guitar. I eventually paid that down."

But that moment of zero-balance paradise didn't last forever. It's a big world, and there's always something more to buy. What are humans if not eager little spenders?

Over the years, Dave's spending seesawed. When his band raked in cash from a concert or he licensed music to a commercial client, he paid off his debt. Between those infusions, he slapped his life on plastic. Unfortunately, the down times have overshadowed the up times. Now, at age forty-four, Dave is struggling to pay off what is a massive amount of debt. On paper, he looks like a reckless spender. But deep down, he knows he's never lived lavishly. After all, he was only charging life's little necessities: a little pizza here, some drinks with friends there, a trip to the drugstore. Somehow, in twenty years' time, those small purchases have added up to something enormous. "The miracle of compound interest," he jokes wryly.

These days, Dave's trying to aggressively pay down his debt—and keep a lid on spending. "I don't normally track my spending, other than estimating it," he says. "But lately I *have* been. I *know* my credit-card bills and rent are my biggest expenses, so I am basically trying to keep my other expenses, like food, drinks, and leisure stuff, very low right now. So I feel like I need to itemize everything or use some software to carefully monitor everything. I probably should!"

We would absolutely agree. Since Dave stays on top of his payments, an inability to make monthly payments and keep his credit intact is not the issue here. However, his spending has an effect on his ability to reduce his debt.

Tracking spending is one of the most powerful ways to keep it under control. And thankfully, there are many easy ways to do that. One of our favorite ways to snap ourselves back to fiscal reality is to spend a little quality time with a financial calculator.

Hugh Chou is a self-proclaimed computer geek and founder of www.hughchou.org, which features numerous financial calculators written and developed by Hugh himself. Hugh is a paragon among savers. He rarely eats out and never, ever buys soft drinks. ("Why pay for sugared water?" is his philosophy.) Though he runs the site as a hobby, the ten thousand hits per day that he generates have catapulted him to a kind of celebrity status among financial geeks. As a result, people contact him constantly for advice about everything from refinancing mortgages to managing spending.

Once, a lady asked him for help figuring out how much she was spending on muffins. Hugh dashed off some code and created Sharon's Muffin Calculator, which calculated that the poor woman was spending the equivalent of a laptop computer per year on muffins! Similarly, Hugh has created calculators that figure out how much you spend on lunch on the go (the Lunch Savings Calculator) and drinks on the town (the Booze/Beverage Savings Calculator).

"Once people see the numbers in front of them, they realize that that's *their* own money. It's a lot more eye-opening," Hugh explains.

And that's what we're going to do here. Open our eyes and take a whole new look at your next account, the Spending Account, and how it fits into the Freelance Finance system.

WHERE YOU'RE AT

Here you are: you now have three brand-new accounts that perhaps you didn't have before. Now, of course, you need to put some money in them. But before the money ends up in your Retirement, Emergency, or Tax accounts—which are being held at online banks—it has to be deposited in your primary Spending Account: the account that you use most, the one that you live with day in and day out. And the one that you may be abusing rather than just using.

In chapter 2 we had you analyze your spending and look at some of your more regular costs. Now we are going to use that information to further refine your relationship to your Spending Account as a part of your new financial lease on life.

Here's what's ahead:

- We will talk about developing a new attitude toward your spending.

- We will discuss setting up and managing your Spending Account.
- We will examine spending trends and your evolving Spending Identity and talk about how they can derail your finances.

REDISCOVERING THE SPENDING ACCOUNT

Let's be honest: spending is a whole helluva lot of fun, isn't it? You see something, it gets you goosed, you take out your wallet, and . . . *voilà!* It's yours forever. You can even take it home right that minute! Fantastic, isn't it? There is nothing like a little immediate gratification to really start your day off right.

If you live in this country and come out from under your rock every once in a while, you probably have a checking account. The question is, are you managing it or simply sucking it dry? Do you view it as an integral part of your wealth-building system, or is it merely a pit stop along the highway that takes you from spending spree to spending spree? This account is valuable and must be treated that way. Deciding when and how much to spend when you do not have a predictable monthly income is one of the most frustrating aspects of streamlining finances as an independent worker. So it is imperative that you view this account as a vital part of the system, not just as a dumping ground for cash until the next big trip to the mall. After all, we all want to get the most entertainment bang for our buck.

The way we see it, this account is not so much a checking

account as it is a Spending Account. Here's the thing: you have an obligation to treat money in this account as nothing short of a sacred object. And not only sacred but finite. Your money is a symbol, an incredibly powerful and tangible symbol, of the sacred and finite object in your life that is, in truth, your time. Unless you've figured out a way to trip up the space-time continuum (and if you have, you probably don't need this book), once your time is spent it is gone—there is no getting it back.

Look at the money you have right now in your Spending Account. Look at it closely. Each and every cent represents a fraction of your time. Why? Because you have traded a part of your life for that money. If you throw it away recklessly, you are essentially devaluing your own time and hence your own efforts. In short, with every pointless and thoughtless dispensing of your cash, you are basically saying your time isn't worth anything.

The Spending Account represents financial potential. It is a sea of choice and priorities for you to navigate. This account has a specific purpose, just like your Retirement or Tax account. The money in there goes to fixed costs, sure, but then . . . well, the rest is up to you. If you hadn't spent that money every day on a seven-dollar lunch out when you could have eaten at home, what could that money have done for you? Over time, quite a bit. Would you have used it to pursue your dreams? To shore up your career, which you say means so much to you? In other words, are you putting your money where your mouth is?

The proper management of the Spending Account can make the difference between wealthy and washed-up. From this point forward, you must no longer look at this account as merely a place that you ransack until there's nothing left, but rather as an incubator for your future fortunes.

SETTING IT UP

You already have a Spending Account—it's probably your primary checking account. If you keep a separate account for your business, then you may have two Spending Accounts—one for the biz and one for yourself. In either case, here are our suggested requirements for the Spending Account:

1. It is held at a brick-and-mortar bank.
2. It has some form of overdraft protection.
3. It provides ATM access.
4. It is linked electronically to your Retirement, Tax, and Emergency accounts.

1. IT IS HELD AT A BRICK-AND-MORTAR BANK

There are a couple of reasons why we suggest setting up your Spending Account at—or moving it to, if need be—a brick-and-mortar bank. First of all, most workers who work gig to gig or client to client have the need to get checks quickly into their account. Some clients are organized enough to have direct electronic deposit, but many are not. Most online banks will allow you to mail in your deposits, but that can add a few days to the amount of time you have to wait for a check to clear and introduces the postal service into the mix, which just presents another opportunity for your check to go missing. (And come on—it takes so long to get the darn things, do you really want that to happen?) We also like the brick-and-mortar bank because it helps you develop a relationship with your bank and possibly your business community. You can walk your deposit in. If there's a problem, there's a person to deal with. They also offer things like notary services. All in all, having one brick-and-mortar bank in your life is the way to go.

2. IT HAS SOME FORM OF OVERDRAFT PROTECTION

We want this account to have overdraft protection. Unsteady cash flow can sometimes lead to ill-timed withdrawals, and the last thing you need are unruly fees making things worse. However, if you are tracking your spending, this should not happen at all. Please, for the love of God, get a spreadsheet, a piece of financial software, the back of a take-out menu—*anything*—and start tracking your spending.

3. IT PROVIDES ATM ACCESS

This account should be the only account with which you have ATM access. Why? Because it should be really, really hard to get money out of your other accounts. This is the account where the money you use day to day is stashed. This is the account you need access to. The others . . . We are trying to protect you from yourself here. If you're trying to cut back on calories, do you keep a stash of cupcakes on hand at all times in an easily accessible pantry? No, you do not. You try to keep the cupcakes out of the house. Throw up a roadblock to ransacking your savings. You shouldn't need to pilfer them anyway, if you are properly managing your money.

4. IT IS LINKED ELECTRONICALLY TO YOUR RETIREMENT, TAX, AND EMERGENCY ACCOUNTS

And finally, this account needs to be linked to your online banks because you will, with every check that comes in the door, be transferring over the appropriate percentages to each of these accounts.

Once you've properly established your account, you will have the wealth funnel in place and be ready to gather up your riches and whisk them away to their proper destinations.

HOW TO USE IT

The money in your Spending Account pays your fixed monthly costs and covers discretionary spending—which you calculated in chapter 2. In other words, your Spending Account holds the money that you get by on day to day, *after* you've taken all your percentages off the top.

How do you spend it carefully? Let's look at the hierarchy of spending:

- Fixed costs (rent, bills, payments on loans, things that must be paid or there are serious consequences). Even late payments can have long-lasting consequences on your financial profile, so keeping these costs on track is an absolute must.
- Discretionary spending. Yes, we realize that some of these expenses are necessary, such as groceries. But *how* you spend your grocery money is a choice and not a fixed cost, right? Think carefully about where those dollars go.

Money should be allotted to the fixed costs first, before the discretionary spending takes place. Since you have worked out what your fixed costs are, you know what you need to have to cover your basics.

BREAKING IT DOWN EVEN MORE: CREATE AN OVERHEAD ACCOUNT

It's one of the best feelings in the world when a big check comes in. This huge number is staring back at you, and you think to yourself, *Ahhhhh . . . what a relief. Now I can relax for a little while. Whew!*

But can you, really?

For those of you who have a more steady stream of income—based on a standard rate you charge clients, for instance, and a base number of clients—then understanding how a large chunk of income affects you is much easier. For those of us who are familiar with the "I'm rich! I'm poor! No wait—I'm rich again!" cash-flow cycle, assessing the real impact of a large inflow can be trickier. What you want to do, obviously, is milk that baby until the cows come home, making sure that you are doing everything you can to ensure the financial health of your career and your life in general.

If you fall into this second category—and this doesn't apply to everyone—you may wish to create what we like to call the Overhead Account.

Early on, when we would receive a larger-than-usual paycheck—say, for a book or ongoing project, as opposed to just an article—we would dutifully take our assigned percentages off the top (sometimes even a little more). We would then look at the amount that was left over in the Spending Account and feel sure that it would last us for, just as an example, about three months.

But it never did.

Why? The money that we thought would cover fixed costs in the months to come was sitting there in our Spending Account with money for groceries, shopping, and entertainment. (Warning! Warning!) It never lasted. It was too hard to tell where the discretionary spending for the present month stopped and the fixed costs for the next month began.

We had an old savings account at our primary bank that we rarely used anymore (because we had created all of our online accounts), and we decided that it had a brand-new purpose: we would designate this as our Overhead Account. From that moment forward, when a big check came in, once we had covered our assigned percentages, we put money to cover fixed costs for upcoming months in the Overhead Account. And then, honestly, we forgot about it. When the first of the month came around, we transferred an amount that would cover our fixed monthly costs back into our Spending Account and went from there. It worked like a charm.

Unless you know for certain that you have more than enough money coming in for the rest of the year, you should take advantage of unusually large paydays to set some money aside to help you cover costs you *know for sure* that you're going to have, like rent or mortgage and car payments. Again, everyone's earning situation is different. But if this has happened to you before, try opening an Overhead Account. If you decide to do so, we suggest choosing a savings account at your brick-and-mortar bank (if you're like us, you may have one that you have somewhat abandoned as you've begun using this system) so that you can get access to the funds quickly and easily.

SPENDING HABITS AND YOUR SPENDING IDENTITY

It's time to take a good look at how well you use what's in your Spending Account. We start by reflecting on a tried-and-true facet of the financial world: compound interest.

Compound interest is routinely described as a miraculous force. Given the way interest builds wealth, that description may well be apt. But what's the opposite of that miracle? Spending. You might say it's one of the world's most *mysterious* forces. Why? Nothing drains away wealth so insidiously.

"A lot of people contact me and say they're out of control," says Hugh, the calculator genius. "They can't figure out why they can't get by in this society. Then they tell me how much they've spent on everything. And I say, 'That's why!' "

The one thing that spending and interest have in common is this: *over time, little things add up to a lot.* This rule is inescapable. Just look at the mathematical logic behind some of Hugh's calculators. Had the muffin lady invested her breakfast money, in ten years she would have saved $5,395.92! Ten years of decompressing with a couple of frosty microbrews—four a week at five dollars a pop—costs $13,081 in the long run. A year of eating modest ($7.50) lunches out costs you a mere $1,500 the first year but adds up to more than $18,866 over ten years, with interest.

Now, are we saying you can't enjoy yourself? Not at all. What we are saying is arm yourself with some knowledge before you spend. If you *really* love your lunches out, if you think they're well worth the price of, say, a Toyota Camry, then go for it. But if most of these meals fail to knock your socks off, then it's time to change the way you spend and invest in some quality time in the kitchen.

We think that budget-killing purchases tend to fall into two main categories: *habit* and *impulse.*

- *Habitual purchases* are things you buy because you have grown accustomed to buying them on an ordinary basis, without questioning why you buy them. Not buying these things often makes you feel uncomfortable, as if you have altered your quality of life. If you use the words "I always" to describe the purchase, it's probably a habit:

"I always stop for coffee in the morning."

"I always have two beers with my friends after work."

"I always eat lunch out."

"I always order appetizers, desserts, and drinks."

"I always take cabs."

"I always drive my own car because I don't like carpooling."

"I always get snacks at the movies."

"I always buy a muffin—or a bagel, a juice, etc.—in the morning."

- *Impulse purchases* are things that you didn't plan to buy but just have to have *now.* The classic example is any must-have you grab while waiting on line to pay at the checkout of any store. Retailers don't display the organic vegetables near the checkout. Instead, they stock things that appeal to the pleasure center of your brain: magazines, candy, gum, flashlight key chains, DVDs, and refrigerator magnets—stuff that looks like the perfect, inexpensive treat for yourself or someone else in your life. Today's gadget-filled universe also coaxes us to "buy on the fly" without ever pulling out cash or plastic. Ringtones, albums, books, videos, TV episodes can all be bought instantly from handheld devices. Impulse purchases can be pricey, too. A pair of leather boots that you didn't anticipate buying but simply must have *now,* for example. Purchases like these can easily ruin your finances.

While some people are made of Teflon, the majority of us are highly susceptible to this kind of buying. There is no easy way to stop reckless spending if you have become accustomed to spending at will for a long time. The only things that help are the two steps we outlined in chapter 2:

- Track every dime you earn and spend. (This is much easier with financial software.)
- Gradually alter your Spending Identity by setting attainable goals for yourself. (Go back to the sheet you created in chapter 2. As you get each line item under control, revise and print out a new Spending Identity sheet to tackle new items.)

What follows are some tips, strategies, and gimmicks for monitoring what's happening in your Spending Account. A lot of these ideas will help you save money. Now, we don't want to make a huge deal about living frugally, because goodness knows all of us have earned the right to do with our money what we wish.

However . . .

One of our favorite books—and one we list in the appendix—is a classic entitled *The Millionaire Next Door.* In it, the authors, who studied the behavior of wealthy people, found that self-employed people were the ones most likely to become millionaires. Hurray! Doesn't that put a smile on your face? But the far more important finding was that these people were extraordinarily frugal. They drove ordinary cars, bought ordinary clothing, and resoled their shoes rather than toss them out. Basically, these millionaires built wealth doing the kinds of things that we have been trained by our spendthrift culture to regard as loser moves. But who's the real loser? The guy who leases the flashy car he can't really afford to buy, carries tens of thousands on his credit card, and pumps no money into his retirement fund—or the guy in the resoled Buster Browns who builds a fortune?

It's a thought worth thinking about as you consider these (non)spending strategies.

ALWAYS BE ANALYZING ("ABA") We get geeky pleasure out of watching how the pie chart on our financial software changes each month to reflect our shifting priorities and behavior. If you're not familiar with them, they look a little like the charts you see on page 178. What we like about them is that you can figure out what your top five or ten costs are at a glance. If you don't analyze your spending on a regular basis, you probably won't catch on to a new habit until it becomes an unshakable one. As we say, we happen to think crunching this kind of data is fun, but we're major dorkchops. If the idea of seeing graphical representations of your spending makes you want to gag, think of them as randomly generated, highly personal, homemade works of art.

KNOW WHAT YOU'RE SPENDING *TODAY* People, is it so crazy to ask you to write down what you intend to buy or spend each morning before you leave the house? Most self-employed people mentally organize their day anyway, whether they know it or not: *I'm working on those sketches for my current project until noon. I have a presentation meeting at 1:30 p.m. Then I take the dry cleaning in. Then the car goes to the garage. And I'm meeting Justin for drinks.* Why couldn't you write this schedule and jot down, in parentheses, what you think you'll be spending on each of these errands, meetings, or social gatherings? You could even add it as a note on your paper, computer, or handheld calendar. Do it for a week. We promise that this exercise will bowl you over. If you don't like what you're about to spend, you have time to sidestep the impending doom. If someone tries to tempt you with a lunch date, you will know at a glance whether or not you're way over the day's intended spending limit.

KNOW THY NEEDS AND WANTS As we've said before, it's easy to confuse *needs* (things that are absolutely necessary for the successful continuation of your life or business) with *wants* (things you'd just love to have or do). If you can't tell the difference immediately, chances are it's a want. It helps to review the wish list you drew up in chapter 4 on a regular basis, eliminating the things that you no longer want, and reprioritizing the remaining ones. You should do this with low-ticket purchases (under $150, say) as well.

GO ON A SHOPPING FAST Sometimes it's helpful to go through an entire twenty-four-hour period without spending a dime. During this time, write down the things that you were tempted to buy, and later evaluate the list rationally. What does the list tell you about yourself? How many of those things are bona fide needs? Can you envision extending the fast to forty-eight or seventy-two hours?

PURGE THOUGHTFULLY Everyone has a place where they tuck away total crap. A closet. A basement room. A storage unit. For some reason, you don't want to part with these items, but you really don't engage with them on a daily basis. Take the time to carefully sort through this stuff, and try to remember what you spent on it. Would you ever spend money on this stuff again? Did you really get that much use out of it? Are you

SPENDING FOR MARCH

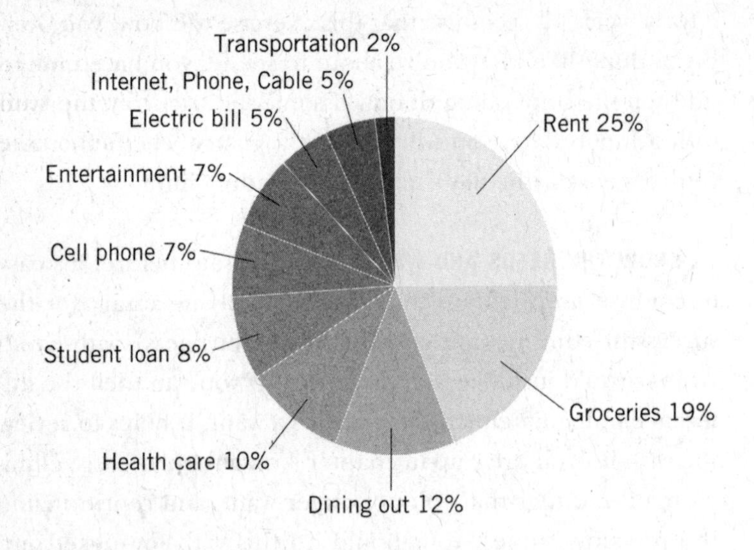

SPENDING FOR JUNE

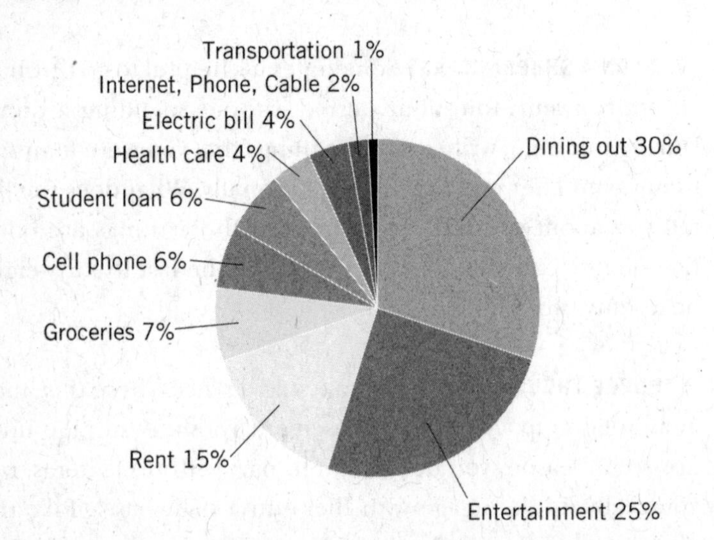

Significant shifts in your spending habits can happen before you notice they're a problem. Here, dining out and entertainment have ballooned to become the two largest spending categories in this person's budget.

frankly surprised by what you have? This exercise is a little like paging through an old diary or journal and being amazed at the now-trivial crises that sapped your energy and consumed your time. Here, you're likely to be blown away by the stuff that sucked your wallet dry. Listen to the past. Now's the time to quit making the same mistakes.

CHANGE YOUR "DESERVE" LANGUAGE *I deserve to eat out. I deserve a new gaming device. I deserve some new office furniture.* Rationalizations like these are hard to argue with. Yes, *everyone* on the planet deserves better than they've got right now. But it's always smarter to stick to your important financial goals. The next time you're tempted by a particularly enticing item, alter the language going on in your head: *I deserve to be debt free. I deserve to pay off this car. I deserve an emergency fund.*

VOTE YOUR DOLLARS More and more, your spending is a political act. If you believe in shopping locally and patronizing local merchants, if you believe in supporting local bookstores, if you value organic groceries, you are "voting" for these things every time you spend a buck. In the same way you wouldn't want to throw away your vote on a lackluster candidate, save your money for the things that matter most to you.

THE POWER AND BEAUTY OF CASH (OR, AN EASY WAY TO STICK IT TO THE MAN)

Our spendy little nation may be breathlessly rushing toward a cashless society, but you don't have to play along. In fact, if you need one more reason to switch back to cash, get this:

every business that accepts debit or credit is paying a percentage of the transaction to the card issuers for the privilege of making that transaction. The percentage *sounds* small, usually no more than 1 percent to 3 percent, but it certainly adds up. Americans spend fifty billion dollars on card-processing fees every year. Now, there's a good argument that if the merchant didn't accept plastic, he wouldn't have gotten your business in the first place. Still, these relentless charges inevitably trickle back to you in the form of costlier goods and services. If you want to stick it to The Man—the big man, not the small businessman—use cash. Your friendly neighborhood merchant will thank you for it.

OLD-SCHOOL SPENDING: THE ENVELOPE SYSTEM

One of the best ways to rein in spending is to use the time-honored Envelope System. This consists of placing fixed amounts of cash—$50, $100, $150—in separate envelopes earmarked for different categories in your weekly or monthly budget. You have one envelope for groceries, one for entertainment, one for dining out, and so on. There are a few rules to this system:

1. Put a week's allotment of cash in each of the envelopes.
2. Pay for everything with cash for the next week.
3. When the envelopes are empty, stop spending. Wait until the following week and a fresh infusion of cash.
4. Write down everything you spend.

That's it. Some may bristle at the thought of tucking spending money in an envelope like a kid heading off to summer camp. But the Envelope System is an effective way of shining a big, bright, impossible-to-ignore light on your spending habits. (In fact, one software company has developed an online program that mimics this system, called Mvelopes. You'll find a listing in the appendix.)

When we experimented with it, the Envelope System taught us quite a bit. At the time, we had weaned ourselves off credit cards but had begun to use our debit cards as if they were distant cousins to plastic. A month of swiping left us wondering why we didn't have enough money in our Spending Account. To get the spending under control, we focused on only two categories that were giving us trouble: food (dining out and groceries) and entertainment. One of us held the food envelope; the other was in charge of the entertainment bucks.

Come Wednesday, Joe would ask, "Hey, why don't we go to the movies?"

And Denise would say, "Nice idea, but we can't afford it."

"How's *that* possible? We had a ton of cash in there just the other day."

"Are you forgetting the play tickets?"

"That show sucked! I'd rather be watching one of these Oscar-nominated movies right about now."

"Wait till next week, buddy-boy."

Yeah, it was shocking to watch how quickly the money flew out the window. But ultimately, *cash grounded us*. Cash made us responsible for every dollar that slipped out of our hands. The system works because it

- keeps you from using credit cards, which are the dirty handmaidens of Satan;

- keeps you from using your debit card profligately;
- forces you to constantly confront your desire to spend and evaluate your choices and your value system.

Listen: as a freelancer, your potential is limitless, but the money you have at any given time is finite. Credit cards trick you into thinking you have an endless supply of money. Debit cards, truth be told, do the same. They breed a hazy understanding of what you really have in the bank, and they impose no limits on you at all, that is until your card is spat back out at you with the stomach-churning message "Insufficient funds."

To get cash, you have to make a point of visiting an ATM. Every time you peek inside that envelope, you are reminded how much has come out, and you are looking right at what you have left. With each and every purchase, as you hand over those dollars and nickels and quarters, you are connected to what you are spending.

Switch back to cash today.

WHAT TO DO

Well, we've added another account to your arsenal. In the next chapter, we're going to walk you through how all of these accounts work together. But first, please make sure you've done the following:

- Make sure, if you have not already, that you have your Spending Account established at a brick-and-mortar bank. Enable electronic links between this bank and each of your new online bank accounts to ensure the easy transferring of funds. (pp. 168–69)

- Look again at your earnings for the last three years. Do you earn roughly the same fees throughout the year from a stable of clients, or does your income vary wildly from job to job? If the latter is your situation, consider establishing an Overhead Account that will help you make the most out of unexpected windfalls. (p. 171)

- Go back to chapter 2 and revisit the Spending Identity Statement. Would your answers be the same now? Have you learned anything new or gained any clarity on your spending habits and priorities in the last several chapters? Complete an updated statement if necessary. (pp. 53–54)

- If you feel like you're always scratching your head in despair, wondering how it's possible that you are just barely scraping by, try the Envelope System for a month (p. 180). Pick an amount that you want to spend on each of three main categories, say, groceries, entertainment, and "incidentals." At the start of each week, place a designated amount in each envelope and make it last for seven days. Every time you spend some of the money, write down on a piece of paper how much you spent and what it was for. Keep that slip of paper and the receipt that goes with it in the related envelope. At the end of the month, ask yourself:

    1. Was this easier or harder than I anticipated?

    2. What did I spend the money on? Would it have been better spent elsewhere?

    3. Are my spending habits in line with my ideals and my dreams?

CHAPTER 8

PUTTING IT ALL TOGETHER

"It's nice to be an independent worker, sure. It's nice when things are *good*," an acupuncturist named James was telling us one day. Both he and his wife, Brenda, a licensed psychologist, are independently employed. So unlike married independent workers who have a spouse with a job that perhaps provides benefits for both of them and maybe even provides enough income to cover basic monthly expenses, both partners are in the same no-benefits boat. (This happens to be the same category we fall into, one we refer to as the "double whammy.") In this case, irony of ironies, James and Brenda are health-care providers who have to provide for their own health insurance.

As a young man, James watched his father, a successful businessman, get laid off in his fifties and never quite recover from it. This experience greatly influenced James's desire to work for himself. The way he saw it, a full-time job with a company was the surest way to a life of job *in*security.

This belief was reinforced early in his own career, when James himself was laid off by a couple of medical facilities where he was working as a technician. After the second layoff, he thought, *That's it! I need a job where I can never be fired.* He decided to return to school to become an acupuncturist. He would forever be self-employed. He'd cultivate his own patients, make his own hours, and be his own boss.

Today James and his wife have a new batch of problems

- established electronic links between all of your bank accounts, including your brick-and-mortar bank;
- begun to train your psyche to believe that you can and will start paying yourself first and building wealth and financial stability.

In this chapter, we are going to walk you through several different payment scenarios to give you a real feel for how you will be managing your money. Once you've stuck with the system for a bit, it will become second nature.

It is crucially important to remember—so we'll say it again—that no two earners are the same. That is one of the major challenges of organizing your finances when you're an independent worker. Some of us are permalancers who have taxes taken out of our pay but still have to cover our own benefits. Some of us work more than one job. Some of us get health care from our spouses (you lucky SOBs . . .). Some of us have never saved before, and some of us have already been paying our estimated taxes. Whatever your individual situation is, the need for top-down organization of your finances is what we all have in common—the need for one system, not a piecemeal approach to saving. So don't look at examples and brush them off, saying to yourself, *Well, that doesn't have anything to do with me.* Maybe that particular example doesn't, but chances are the strategy and philosophy behind the approach do. So hang in there.

SCENARIO 1: BASIC CASH FLOW

In this example, we are assuming that you need to save for taxes, retirement, and emergency accounts. Read this all the way through and think to yourself how you might adjust it for your particular situation. We'll go into more detail about how to do that in chapter 10. For example, if you are a permalancer and have taxes taken out, you can adjust the percentages here based on the accounts you have already created for yourself, or, if part of your income is completely freelance, apply this approach to those checks in particular. If you work for cash, you're tracking that in your cash bag, yes? The same exact approach applies.

Let's begin.

A check of a modest amount arrives at your home.

1. Stand tall, pound your fist in the air, and scream, "Yesss!!"
2. Deposit the check into your Spending Account held at your local bank. (This account should now be linked to your online bank.)
3. Once the check clears, transfer 10 percent, for example, into your Holy Trinity of online bank accounts in the following fashion:
   - Send 3 percent to your Emergency Account.
   - Send 4 percent to your Taxes Account.
   - Send 3 percent to your Retirement Account.
4. Leave the other 90 percent of the check in your Spending Account.
5. Depending on how much money is left over, use that money to *first* pay for your current fixed monthly costs. If you are toward the end of a month, use it to pay for the following month's fixed monthly costs. (You should

now know exactly what this amount is if you've done the work in chapter 2.)

6. If there is still money left over, use that remaining money for discretionary spending. For this example, we are assuming that the amount received is not enough to pay for several months' worth of costs, a situation we address in greater detail in scenario 2, on page 195.

7. With each new payment, lather, rinse, and repeat.

Now, if you have been paying attention, you will notice that 10 percent total—and a measly 4 percent designated for taxes—is not very much. You're absolutely right. Well done. However, ten is a nice round number and makes it easy for us to explain things to you. More important, if you have never, ever taken money out of your checks to set aside for taxes or emergencies or retirement, this is an easy way to start. You won't feel a thing.

A QUICK NOTE ON PERCENTAGES

Yes, math. No whining—this is a cakewalk. All you need to figure this out is a calculator and maybe a paper and pen.

So in keeping with this particular example, let's say you're a cabinet maker who gets a check for $2,200. You are just starting out on this new adventure in saving and paying yourself first, and you are feeling pretty shaky and quaky about taking this money right off the top before you've had a chance to go out and celebrate the fact that your client paid up by buying yourself a nice dinner. But you are committed and have decided to start with the 10 percent allotment shown in the example above as a way to ease yourself into things.

For all of you who have happily decided to make high-school math a thing of the past, here's a quick refresher. To calculate a percentage, do the following:

1. Convert the percentage into a decimal.
    - Write the percentage as a whole number with the decimal point following it.
    - Move the decimal point two places to the left.
2. Multiply that decimal by the total amount of the check.
3. Repeat with the other percentages.

Just like this:

Check amount:	$2,200
Amount going to Emergency Account:	3%
Write 3% as a whole number:	3.
Move the decimal point:	.03
Multiply:	2,200 x .03 = 66
You have your total:	$66

One more time, just to make sure . . .

Amount going to Tax Account:	4%
Write 4% as a whole number:	4.
Move the decimal point:	.04
Multiply:	2,200 x .04 = 88
Your total is:	$88

The same applies for two-digit percentages:

10% = 10. = .10

15% = 15. = .15

Alternatively, you may do the following keystrokes on a calculator, if it has a "%" key. Let's say we want to take 15 percent of $1,700. Just type "1700 x 15% =" and you will get your answer.

Here endeth the math lesson.

Let's take a look at the chart on page 192 for a visual depiction of where your money is going. That's it, folks. It's that simple. The only thing holding you back is the time needed to form some good habits. But this is just a start. In the future, you will need to increase the total you are saving from 10 percent to 15 percent or 20 percent and eventually more. Remember—that's what would be coming out of these checks if you were working for The Man. Now you have to be The Man—or The WoMan. You know what we're going to say next: treat yourself the way a good employer would treat you. But seriously, look at those numbers. That sixty-six dollars that went to the Emergency Account is equal to a night out for a lot of people. Just one night out. Some shoes. That membership at the Y that you never use. Get the picture? You can squeeze savings out of your income. You just have to be sure to get that money into savings before your Dionysian alter ego gets ahold of it and takes it out on the town to whoop it up.

WHERE YOUR MONEY IS GOING

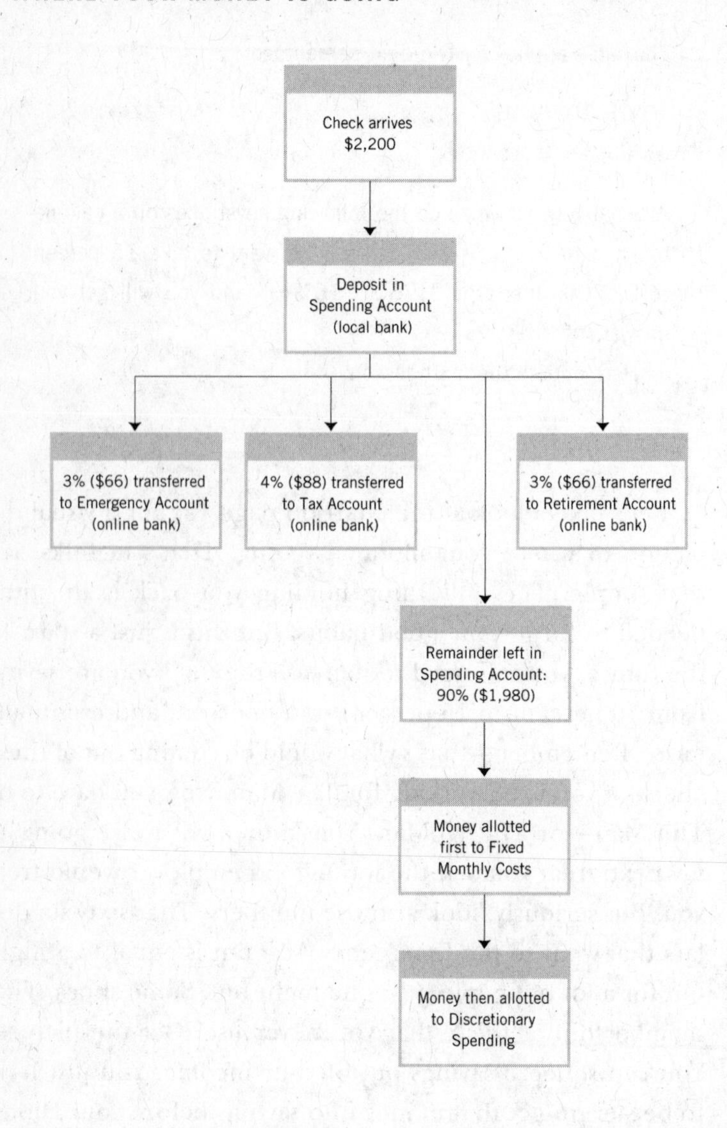

THE POWER OF SMALL

At first glance, it might seem ridiculous to start with such small numbers. You might be thinking, *To hell with 10 percent! I'll save 30 percent!* Well, bully for you! The truth is, you probably ought to be saving at least 30 percent. (Taxes alone will run you 15 percent to 30 percent annually, depending on your income.) However, if you have a poor track record at saving money, it's probably wiser to start with more manageable percentages. If you start high, you may be appalled by how much money you're *not* getting to spend from each paycheck, and you'll be more likely to abandon the system. But if you start low—so low that you barely feel it—you'll train yourself to appreciate the fact that you can indeed spare to save more.

Small percentages can inspire you.

They help you build confidence in your ability to save money and reinforce the notion that you have the discipline to save well. Building up your tolerance to saving is a little like the story of the boiled frog. Drop one into a pot of boiling water and it hops right out. But put one in tepid water and heat it up slowly to the boiling point and it ends up nicely cooked—and its little juicy legs end up on your plate drizzled with butter, if you're into that kind of thing. Be that frog. Let the savings heat up around you without much fuss. Trust us: in time you will happily increase the percentage. Start small and work yourself up until you're smokin'!

IT ALL ADDS UP

Let's look at how the Power of Small would work for you over a year's time and take a closer look at how raising your percentages can have even more impact on your savings.

Say you made a total of $53,000 last year, from a total of eighteen different checks and cash in tips from a second job. The first check that comes in is for $800.

You do your math based on the 10 percent breakdown above:

3 percent to Emergency Account = $24

4 percent to Tax Account = $32

3 percent to Retirement Account = $24

"My savings will never amount to anything this way," you say. True, you do need to up your percentages. But look at what happens with the next check, which clocks in at $4,000:

3 percent to Emergency Account = $120

4 percent to Tax Account = $160

3 percent to Retirement Account = $120

Hmmmm . . . now you have almost $200 in your Emergency Account—and you never even had an Emergency Account before. It starts to add up.

Here is how the savings would look after one year, depending on how much you decided to set aside for different circumstances:

	10% TOTAL	20% TOTAL	30% TOTAL
Emergency	$1,590 (3%)	$2,650 (5%)	$2,650 (5%)
Tax	$2,120 (4%)	$5,300 (10%)	$7,950 (15%)
Retirement	$1,590 (3%)	$2,650 (5%)	$5,300 (10%)
TOTAL	**$5,300**	**$10,600**	**$15,900**

As you can see, the savings really add up—and we're not even allowing for the modest interest that many online banks offer.

Let's say you were saving 30 percent. At the end of the first year, you would have a total of $7,950 in your Emergency and Retirement accounts, plus the moderate interest that would have accrued along the way depending on when deposits were made and what their individual amounts were.

The very next year, let's assume you earn 3 percent interest. This is low, yes, but not bad for a basic online bank account—and much more than you would probably get at a traditional bank. After one year, you would make $238.50. The following year, another $245.66 would be added to that. And in the third year, add another $253.02. After just three years, that original $7,950 would have grown to $8,687.18 without your lifting a finger. *And* we're not even taking into account all of the money that you would have been adding into the account along the way.

What is also obvious, of course, is how considerable the savings can be when you start upping your percentages. At 30 percent, you are making significant strides toward covering all of your bases and you will get to your goals faster, which can have a *huge* impact on your attitude toward saving. This is your goal: to take as much off the top of your paycheck as possible so that you can begin to really soak up the juicy benefits and peace of mind that come along with building your financial cushion and hopping into the driver's seat when it comes to your money and your career.

Now let's look at some other possible scenarios that you might encounter.

SCENARIO 2: USING THE OVERHEAD ACCOUNT

In this example, we are going to examine a situation that many of us fall into—the arrival of the bigger-than-usual payday. It's hardly a bad thing when a big, whopping check comes in the door. In fact, it can render even the most stone-faced, worrywart of freelancers virtually slaphappy at the thought of not having to worry about money . . . at least for a little while.

The trouble with big checks is that they distort our idea of how well we're doing overall. Three prosperous months in a row and we soon lose sight of the fact that we could, conceivably, hit a dry month. "Then you're kicking yourself for spending all that extra money," says Sherrill St. Germain, a financial planner with New Means Financial Planning in Hollis, New Hampshire. "It helps to pull back and look at the big picture. How does your earning look from fifty thousand feet up? Some money comes in? Great. Put some aside for the IRS. Save some. Then ask yourself: How does this fit into my overall earning for the year?"

Maximizing the impact of a windfall payment can help you get by in lean times. Here's the way to pull it off.

Let's say an artist named Carly gets a major check for a design that she licensed to a department store and that the store has decided to use in several commercial spots. *Cha-ching!* It would seem foolish for her to leave all that money sitting in the Spending Account, right? She knows that based on prior experience and plain old human nature, the balance in her Spending Account would drop faster than a taffeta formal on prom night. We don't want that to happen now, do we? So she's going to take a shot at using an Overhead Account.

The check is for sixteen thousand dollars. Once Carly finally comes to and picks herself up off the floor, she does the following math.

First, she takes out her standard 10 percent.

3% to Emergency Account	=	$480
4% to Tax Account	=	$640
3% to Retirement Account	=	$480

She transfers the money and is left with $14,400 in her Spending Account. This miraculous happening takes place on the twenty-third of the month, and all of her bills for the current month are paid. She's getting antsy . . . that fancy mobile phone she wanted feels within reach. The new desk . . . But wait—she's not done.

Because she dutifully did the work in chapters 2 and 3, she knows that her fixed monthly costs are $3,700. She also knows that she is not expecting another payment for at least ninety days, and that's only if the client pays on time. She divides the $14,400 by $3,700 and comes up with 3.9. She will need to pay her rent and other fixed monthly costs for the coming month in just over a week, so that leaves 2.9. She can easily put aside two months' worth of fixed monthly costs in the Overhead Account and still have some money left over. She can do the following:

- calculate the minimum amount of discretionary income she needs for those two months (to cover groceries, etc.) and put that aside as well;
- divide the money equally between her Emergency, Tax, and Retirement accounts, since she is not currently investing a very large percentage;
- make a large payment to her credit card.

What Carly decides to do is based on a number of items, not the least of which is how much work she has lined up. If cli-

CARLY'S CHECK

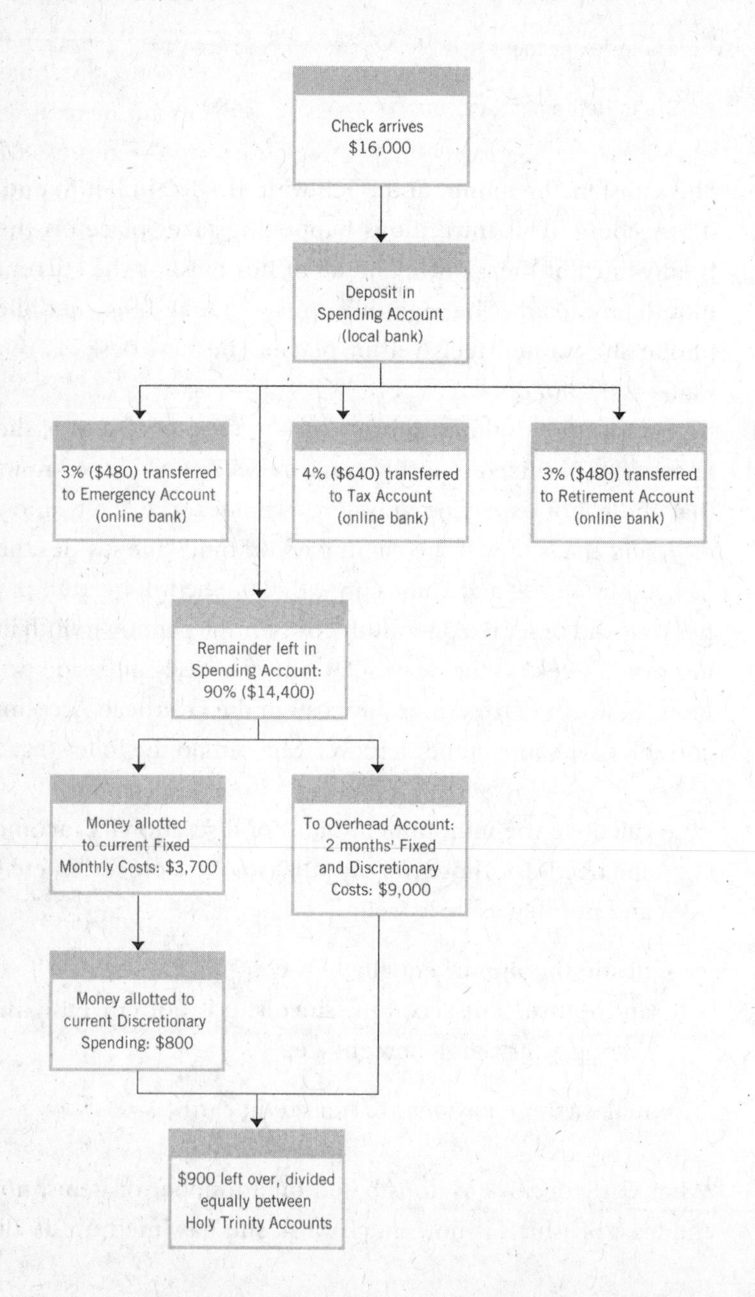

ents are scarce, the first choice is probably the best. When it's time to pay another month's worth of bills, Carly simply transfers that money over from her Overhead Account into her Spending Account and she's good to go. For the next three months—and this is the really wonderful part—she just focuses on her work and her life. She will almost forget that the money is there. She will look at what is in her Spending Account as if it represents all the money she has to spend. When new checks come in, she can continue the process, and the confidence she gains will have her increasing her percentages in no time.

WHAT TO DO WHEN . . .

Once you have set up the Holy Trinity accounts, they do their job so well that you only have to check in on them a couple of times a year. But there are one or two things you might want to keep in mind. Let's take a look at some tips for their proper care and feeding.

MANAGING THE EMERGENCY ACCOUNT

The Emergency Account is the one account that theoretically has a finite ending. The Retirement Account goes on forever, or until you retire. The Tax Account is, in the words of the old saying, as sure as death. But your Emergency Account has a fixed goal in sight. Once you reach that goal, you can shift that percentage of your savings to other financial goals. We'll talk more about this in chapter 10, but for now, it's important to know that you will not be saving for emergencies forever.

When should you stop funding this account? Experts recommend that you keep three to six months' living expenses in emergency money. But as we've said before, we think independent workers should have at least six, maybe more. In tough economic times, you might want more than even nine months' worth socked away. In truth, only you can decide the number.

Just remember: after you've maxed out your Emergency Account, if you withdraw funds from it, you need to readjust your percentages and pay yourself back. You can refer back to page 130 for a refresher on using the Emergency Account, and we will get into adjusting your percentages in chapter 10: "Growing the System."

MANAGING THE TAX ACCOUNT

Throughout the year, you'll be making disbursements from your Tax Account each time you pay your estimated taxes. After all quarterly taxes and year-end taxes are paid, you'll want to assess how well you did saving for your taxes and make any adjustments in the following year.

- If you owed more money on April 15 than you had in your Tax Account, you will want to *increase* the percentage that you are sending to this account.

- If you had just enough money, congratulations. You figured your percentages perfectly.

- If you had a sizable amount of money left over, you may wish to *decrease* the percentage you are sending to this account if you expect about the same level of income and deductions next year. What should you do with the extra money remaining in your account? You could contribute more to your SEP, Roth, or other tax-advantaged accounts, if possible. You could leave it in your Tax Account for the next year. You could add the money to your Emergency Account if it has not yet reached your goal level. Or you could go on a spending spree. Just kidding!

MANAGING THE RETIREMENT ACCOUNT

You can invest in a mutual fund for as little as one dollar at some firms. But if you intend to invest your money with a financial-services company that has an opening account minimum, such as three thousand or five thousand dollars, you'll need to keep your money in the Retirement Account at your online bank until you've reached this goal. (Note: in our fifty-three-thousand-dollar example above, the saver easily would have saved enough in the first year to open an account.) When you hit that goal, you can transfer the money from the online bank to the new account. After that, you can send in money whenever you have it. Contributions to established accounts can be as low as fifty to a hundred dollars at most firms.

If this sounds like you no longer need a Retirement Account at your bank, think again. It still makes more sense to collect your retirement money first in a bank account before sending it on to a brokerage house. Why? Because the tax-advantaged retirement savings accounts we mentioned in chapter 6—SEPs, Simple IRAs, Solo 401(k)s—have tricky contribution limits. You are better off delaying deposits until your tax guru clearly determines how much money you can send to each. Exceptions to this rule: if you are eligible for a Roth IRA, you can always put the maximum in your account without having to determine how this impacts your taxes. Similarly, you can contribute to a taxable brokerage account at any time. But it's best to fund the tax-advantaged accounts first.

SUMMING IT UP

Funding your accounts on a per-check basis using percentages couldn't be easier. In time, you'll develop a sweet little routine of calculating your percentage as each payment comes in and sending your savings to each of your accounts. We predict you will undergo a strange conversion. Instead of constantly dreaming what you can spend your money on, you'll obsess instead about how much you'll be able to save. In other words, money will no longer signify material possessions but the persistent march toward realistic goals.

Now, while some enterprising (freelance) software developers might write nifty plug-ins or apps to help them perform all the steps we've mentioned in this chapter—hint, hint—the majority of us will still need to do this by hand. It will take a little bit of discipline, but if you let it become a habit, you'll soon be looking forward to doing it every time.

You will find over time that your success with this system still boils down to the three main ingredients we covered in the first part of this book:

- how much you make
- how much you spend
- how much you owe

No doubt some of you reading this are screaming: *But there's no way I can save 10, 20, 30 percent or more! How on earth will I ever be able to live?!*

Listen to yourself: you can't save 10 percent?

Come, now! How did you live when you had a "real" job and the boss was helping himself to your money and sending you home with 60 percent or 70 percent of your income? You probably lived just fine on your take-home pay. But when you became a freelancer, you fell into the trap that we all do when faced with the prospect of unsullied riches. You let your lifestyle slowly creep far outside your means.

Sorry to be so blunt, but in the end, the real choices are always the same:

- make more
- spend less
- save always

The Holy Trinity, the per-check percentage system, the swift and steady flow of cash to accounts—all this works well if you let it become part of your life. The only thing that threatens to upset this tidy system is an onerous four-letter word: D-E-B-T.

WHAT TO DO

Finally, we're cooking with gas, as they say. You've now seen how it all fits together. Here are some tasks that will help drive it home and make it stick.

- Work with your new percentages. Start *now.* What is the amount of the next check that you are anticipating receiving? Based on the percentages you have chosen, compute the amounts now that will go into your various accounts. Get mentally ready to transfer the funds the minute they come in the door. (p. 194)

- Get psyched. Look at what you made last year. Take 15 percent of the total. Now go to one of the dandy online calculators we recommend in the appendix, and plug in that amount. How much would you have in ten, fifteen, or twenty years if that 15 percent savings were invested and earning around 8 percent interest?

CHAPTER 9

PAYING OFF DEBT

Dave, the musician from chapter 7, may not know the exact date that his credit cards got out of hand, but he's pretty clear on how it happened. "Basically, for almost the entire span of the nineties, I didn't have very much credit-card debt," he says. "I always had less than five thousand dollars on my cards. But in the last five years, I feel like, along with millions of others, I'm part of a microcosm of this larger, crazy, quasi-Ponzi debt scheme thing that seems to be plaguing everybody."

Dave sees lots of other independent workers—Web developers, graphic designers, and so on—in the same boat. They've all got exciting, dynamic careers in expensive cities—and they're all dealing with inconsistent cash flow. Hovering over them all is a predatory financial system that ensnares them in a cruel, Faustian bargain. Make a mistake, and you're in credit-card hell.

"Things were going pretty well for a while," Dave continues, "but then at some point, I was having some cash-flow problems. I haven't been late on any payments, but now I have huge balances."

In the past, when his cards got out of hand, Dave was fortunate to reap small financial windfalls that enabled him to pay down his credit-card debt. Once, for instance, he licensed some of his music to a company that used it for a television commercial and paid him a whopping twenty thousand dollars! (Irony of ironies, the client was a credit-card company.) Another year, a multinational bank—what is it with Dave and huge financial institutions?—paid him twenty-five thousand dollars for another piece of music. But such windfalls haven't happened recently. As his debt-to-credit ratio rose, Dave's credit score dropped. His credit-card companies perceived him as a risk and proceeded to jack up the interest rates on his cards. Dave thinks about getting a "real" job to help pay down some of his debt, but that would eat into the time he devotes to his musical work. It takes *time* to compose and perform music well, just as it takes time to choreograph a dance routine, see patients, design a functional Web site, or write and manage a successful blog. If he goes for the bucks, he loses out on the thing that matters most to him.

This trap, insists Dave, is common for anyone who works gig to gig.

"People who are freelance, everyone is going for the big score," he says. "Sometimes you get things, sometimes you don't. I like the freelance lifestyle, but there's not a lot of work right now. It's very stressful. I haven't had a real job in fifteen years. What can I submit myself for?"

Dave's cyclical struggle with debt feels terribly familiar, whether or not you happen to be freelance. Remember your middle-school and high-school English classes? Teachers would trot out tales from Greek and Roman mythology, applauding the timelessness of their themes and relating them to modern-day quagmires facing humans. If we were to choose one myth that brings home the misery of debt, it would have to be the Greek tale of Sisyphus. Sisyphus was condemned to push an enormous boulder up a steep hill, only to have it roll back down once he reached the top, forcing him to start the whole painfully exhausting and futile exercise all over again.

Is this what paying down your debt feels like to you?

It can be a terribly Sisyphean exercise, paying and paying and paying only to have any gains that you've made rolled back further by ill-informed spending, unexpected emergencies, escalating bank charges, or any combination of the three. Debt is by far the biggest threat to both your career and your stability and stands between you and your success. If you've taken time to look at how much interest you're still paying year after year on items that may be long gone—or meals long digested—and watched your balance dip only to rise again, you see why credit cards are also called "revolving" debt. You pay, you pay, you spend a little, you pay some more, and all the while you never seem to see that balance go down very much. It's like being stuck in a revolving door: you keep going around and around, never really getting anywhere, and all the while the entire experience just makes you want to jump out and puke.

LEARNING TO HATE DEBT

If "bad" debt is a major issue for you, and you need to give yourself a little psychological boost before you are ready to strap in and begin tackling it, why not learn to hate credit and charge cards and the system behind them?

First, think about all the ridiculous charges that card issuers concoct and the seemingly limitless reasons they invent to raise your interest rates. Think about how much money they take in, the ridiculous bonus packages they pay their executives, all the while seeking federal bailouts. Who's bailing *you* out?

So is it working yet? Are you getting adequately ticked? Come on, try it—it's fun! Think about the effect that debt is having on your life and your overall mood. Then think about the banks and credit-card companies that are getting rich off your misery. Do you have to take responsibility for charging all of those items on your card? Absolutely. You most definitely do. But we would also argue that many credit-card issuers have evolved, unchecked, into big, hairy beasts that are nothing short of predatory. So take responsibility for your part, yes, and then you can still muster a little rage at the system if it's going to help you get your finances back on track.

As we've said before, spending is becoming more and more like a political act. Where do you want your money to go? To faceless, bloodsucking banking corporations or to your own future and the future of those closest to you? To causes that resonate with you on a personal level or to line the ever-expanding pockets of wealthy financiers?

You took a pretty close look at your debts and interest rates in chapter 3. You ranked them, analyzed them, came to terms with them. In this chapter we are going to plug that information into the system. In chapter 3 you also committed to paying off your debts in an order that makes sense: focusing on the debt with the highest interest rate first and working your way down the list (unless there's a small balance you want to prune first to give yourself a boost). Now we are going to finesse your approach by showing you how to find the money and ways to pay down your debt as efficiently and quickly as possible.

As we've said before, debt is sucking the money from your present to pay for your past at the expense of your future. It's time to put it in its proper place.

HIERARCHY OF DEBT

Hugh Chou told us he is always shocked by how many people inquire about ways to pay off their mortgages, despite the fact that they have huge amounts of credit-card debt. We think we know why this happens: credit-card debt seems so normal that many people can't imagine themselves without it. Paying off your house is a tempting and noble goal, no doubt. But placing a mortgage ahead of getting rid of thousands of dollars of credit-card debt is not the way to go. Do *not* make extra efforts to pay off "good debt" while you still have major credit-card debt.

Right about now you may be asking yourself, *What comes first? Should I pay off my debt or save for taxes, retirement, and emergencies?*

The answer is yes.

You have to save for retirement.

You have to save for your taxes.

You have to save for emergencies.

You have to pay down your debt.

We think it's important for you to make an effort to do *all* of these. When people advise putting off this or that priority in order to pay down debt, the advice is often sound. It just doesn't take into account the independent worker's lifestyle. A traditional employee can postpone saving for retirement for a little while if he already has a 401(k) at the office. A freelancer cannot. A traditional worker doesn't have to think about setting aside money for taxes. An independent worker absolutely must. Got it?

That said, we realize that it is not always possible to tackle everything if large debt is causing major problems in your life. Let's take a look at three of these priorities and see if we can come up with a strategy.

1. TAXES

If you do not have taxes taken out of your pay, then saving for taxes is nonnegotiable. "But I have so much debt . . ." you cry. OK. But you'll probably end up with more debt if you don't set aside enough money for your taxes. You do not want to end up with IRS-imposed penalties because you didn't pay on time, didn't file on time, or decided you needed an extended payment plan. You have to set aside money for your taxes, period. Do not screw around with this one. Doing so is a guaranteed shortcut to hell. If you are a permalancer who has taxes collected at the office, mazel tov. If *all* your income is already being taxed by an employer, then cross taxes off your list. Otherwise, you must pay into the Tax Account with every check or bundle of cash that comes in the door, no matter what. *No matter what.*

2. EMERGENCIES

By now you know that the Emergency Account takes on great importance for the independent worker. Does it make sense to scrimp and save to get your sixth month of expenses in your Emergency Account while ten thousand dollars' worth of debt at 18 percent is staring you in the face? From a strict accounting perspective, it does not. However, in a shaky economy, you may want to build up your Emergency Account by paying less to your credit cards. You must assess this.

- Are your work and pay unsteady?
- Is your Emergency Account small or nonexistent?
- Have you noticed a drop-off in assignments, projects, or clients?
- Are you fearful that you won't have enough money to pay bills if work dries up?

If your answer to most of these is yes, postpone paying your debt down aggressively, and build up your Emergency Account instead. If you feel reasonably secure in your work life, then make sure you save at least one month's worth of expenses in your Emergency Account before embarking on an aggressive debt-reduction program.

3. RETIREMENT

Again, if you do not save for your retirement, no one else will. But if your debt is out of control, you may need to devote a smaller percentage of every check to your Retirement Account until you get your debt to a manageable amount. We can hear you now: *But paying down debt may take forever at the expense of my retirement.* Let's hope not. If you commit to paying the debt down aggressively, you will be ramping up your retirement savings in no time. And remember: it does not make mathematical (ugh! math!) sense to invest a large percentage in a retirement account that, on average, may bring you 8 percent, if you have thousands in debt financed at 23 percent interest. Your debt is already taking a toll on your retirement—and your emergency savings and your future plans.

If your situation is so dire that you can't imagine setting aside money for taxes or emergencies while paying even a cent more than the very minimum on your credit cards, then we will do our best to help you. Please just admit to yourself that what you are doing now is not working. Something has to give. The debt monster is not a friend to the independent worker. The teeny, tiny insignificant minimums that card issuers require you to pay are so tempting and make you feel like you're actually handling your debt. You're not. This is why debt is so deadly. Seriously—do you think they're letting you pay those minuscule amounts out of the goodness of their stone-cold, money-grubbing hearts?

And yes, all of this—paying taxes, paying down debt, saving for retirement—is a lot easier if you have a fixed, reliable income. But you don't, so get over it.

Once you accept that things need fixing—and we're not saying beat yourself up here, we're just saying *get real*—you must also realize that the extent to which you will take from emergencies and retirement to pay down debt will depend on your specific circumstances. You must be realistic with yourself about your circumstances as you decide how much you can pay.

As we get ready to help you determine that, let's talk about debt as—you guessed it—a percentage.

THE PERCENTAGE PLUS PAYMENT PLAN

There are many ways to pay off debt. Many people do it in a fairly scattered manner—a little here, a little there, with no real approach.

One of the fastest ways to get debt under control is to do as we outlined in chapter 3: slay the top dragon—the credit card with the highest interest rate—first. When he's gone, you slay the next in line. As you march down the line, the money you save on interest is helping you pay off more of the remaining debt. To guide you in your ruthless extermination of these dragons, do what the credit-card companies do: obsess about the percentages.

Here's the ideal payoff strategy. In the first month, strive to pay as much as you can of the total balance on the card with the highest interest. Pay the bare minimum to all the others on your list. In month two, pay what you paid the first month to your top card, *even though the balance has dropped.* And continue paying the minimum on all your other cards. Keep doing this until the top card is completely paid off.

Where will this money come from? Since you are already using the Freelance Finance system, you can take a percentage of every check that comes in the door to fund some of these credit-card payments. This will help you pay down in a fixed, prioritized manner each month. You're not sending a mere twenty-five or a hundred dollars. What you're sending is directly related to your earning. And that amount is dedicated to debt reduction before it can be spent on unnecessary purchases. On top of this percentage, send whatever bonus cash you can scrimp, save, or earn—either by downsizing your lifestyle or by coming up with creative ways to earn extra money. We call this the Percentage Plus Payment Plan.

Say you make about $44,000 a year and have $12,000 on a single credit card at a rate of 15 percent. Your minimum payment is $300 per month. Making minimum payments only (and the payments get smaller the more payments you make), it will take you—brace yourself—twenty-seven years and three months to be rid of your debt. And what's more, you will pay $11,757.85 in interest.

But if you kept paying $300 per month even as the company continued to lower your minimum monthly payment, you would pay off your card in four years and seven months and pay $4,739.59 in interest.

Now, if you were to pay 10 percent of the total ($1,200) and kept paying the same $1,200 every month until you extinguished the debt, it would take you eleven months to pay off your credit card and you would have paid $900.37 in interest.

We can hear you already, howling at the pages of this book: *Ten percent of my credit card debt is $1,000 a month. There's no way I can pay all this! I have other bills! I have a life! I don't earn enough.*

Relax. First of all, 10 percent is an ideal if you want to get rid of your debt quickly. Something to strive for. Second, we think *anything* is possible if you put your mind to it. Remember the blogger J. D. Roth from chapter 2? When he committed to paying off his thirty-five-thousand-dollar debt, he wiped it out completely in thirty-nine months. That means he plunked down, on average, about nine hundred dollars a month for three and a quarter years until he paid it off. Is nine hundred dollars 10 percent of thirty-five thousand? No, it's not. But it's a sizable commitment. He was earning only about forty-two thousand dollars a year at the time, so he was basically shelling out the equivalent of a quarter of his income each month. He accomplished this remarkable feat by living frugally, eating meals at home or brown-bagging, and selling off his useless crap, the very same crap, we might add, that had gotten him into debt in the first place. "I used eBay, craigslist, the neighborhood garage sale, anything I could find," he told us, "to generate some quick cash, and all of that cash went to pay off my debt."

So . . . no more excuses. If you want to pay off your debt, find a way to come up with the money. And yes, you will have to change your lifestyle to do it—you can start by hiding those cards.

MAKING PAYMENTS

The two big questions: how much can you really afford to pay and where is it coming from? There is no one answer that applies to everyone, but here are some steps that you can take that should make choosing a paycheck percentage—which you will then supplement with whatever discretionary spending and other funds you can scrape together—a little easier:

1. You know what your total debt is. Can you afford, from your discretionary funds, to pay at least 10 percent of the balance on the card with the highest interest rate and still pay the minimum on all the others? If the answer is yes, then by all means do that. Thereafter, whenever you make your payments, send in the same amount you sent in month one to your highest card and the minimums on any others. If you can do this, you may not need to implement the Percentage Plus Payment Plan.

2. If you are not able to take the approach outlined above . . .

   a. The card with the highest interest rate will enter the Percentage Plus Payment Plan. From now on, take a percentage of all your earnings (checks or cash) and set it aside in a new, separate account at your online bank until it's time to pay your credit-card bill. (For more on choosing a percentage, see pages 217–19).

b. When the bill is due, assess: with the funds in your Percentage Plus Account and additional discretionary funds, can you pay 10 percent to the top card and minimums on the others? If so, do that. If not, you may want to increase the percentage you are saving from each paycheck. Do the best you can.

3. As each card is paid off, move to the next card on the list and single it out for the Percentage Plus treatment.
4. Remember: if you cannot make at least the monthly minimum payments on all of your cards, contact a credit counselor. Do not start moving money around like a Turks and Caicos banker.

If this sounds confusing, or if 10 percent to your top card seems impossible, keep reading, and we'll walk you through a sample debt-pay-down scenario. But first . . .

SOME HINTS FOR FINDING THE MONEY

It's hard for all of us to imagine coming up with the money to pay off sizable or massive debts. If you haven't carefully analyzed your monthly costs, you will automatically assume that you "have to" spend what you are currently spending, that there's nowhere else to cut. But when people successfully pay off debt, they do so by doing four important things.

- They lower their overhead (i.e., fixed monthly costs).
- They dramatically rein in discretionary spending.

- They focus on raising their income.
- They defer dreams.

We would argue that you should do all of these things and more. If you're doubtful about the "more," here's what we're talking about.

SQUEEZE IT FROM THE HOLY TRINITY

If you have a big freakin' mountain of debt, you will probably want to divert a portion of the total percentage you're sending to these three accounts to your credit cards. We're not against doing this. We just want you to do it carefully and consistently. For starters, you know you can't divert money from your Tax Account unless you know beyond a shadow of a doubt that you are oversaving to pay your taxes. That leaves the Emergency and Retirement accounts. If you have nothing in your Emergency Account, we think you absolutely must continue contributing to this account until you have at least one month's worth of fixed costs. Once you have that, you may reduce further payments to the Emergency Account until you have your debt under control. But once it is under control, start contributing to your Emergency Account again. What is "under control"? Let's define it as being able to pay 10 percent of your *total* credit-card debt without blinking an eye.

Similarly, you can reduce—but not eliminate entirely—contributions to your Retirement Account. Some advisers say it's OK to stop contributing entirely, but those who do are often speaking generally and are directing their comments to employed people who already have a 401(k) at work. The Retirement Account is simply too important for an independent worker to eliminate entirely while paying down debt.

So how might an amended Holy Trinity look? We envision something like the following chart. Remember, these are sample percentages, not *suggested* percentages. And we are assuming . . .

- that the economy is not in meltdown and this saver is confident of steady work;
- that this particular saver feels comfortable saving one month's expenses to her Emergency Account;
- that she is starting from zero in her Emergency Account.

ACCOUNTS	DESIRED PERCENTAGES	DESIRED PERCENTAGES (DEBTOR STYLE)
Emergency	7.5%	3%
Taxes	15%	15%
Retirement	7.5%	5%
Credit cards	N/A	7%

In this example, notice that the saver's priorities, as indicated by the percentages, are the following: taxes first, credit cards second, retirement third, and emergency fourth. Once this saver has one month's worth of fixed costs in her Emergency Account, she may choose to stop paying into that account and send it all to her credit cards, like so:

ACCOUNTS	DESIRED PERCENTAGES (DEBTOR STYLE)
Emergency	0%
Taxes	15%
Retirement	5%
Credit Cards	10%

Of course, 10 percent of each paycheck may not be enough in a month's time to pay 10 percent to your highest credit card and the minimums on the others. The difference will have to come out of your discretionary funds. This is the "plus" part of the Percentage Plus Payment Plan. If, however, saving 10 percent from each paycheck *is* enough to cover your payments but not yet enough to pay 10 percent to *all* your cards (not just the top one), you will still want to send as much additional money as you can. Where will you get it? Read on.

REDUCE FIXED OVERHEAD COSTS

Savvy folks know that fixed costs aren't so fixed after all. Most of them reflect choices you have made about the kind of lifestyle you want to enjoy. The easiest items to cut are things such as pricey gym memberships, cable TV packages, and entertainment subscriptions such as Netflix, TiVo, and satellite radio. These things are begging to be trimmed. But other fixed costs can be negotiated. If you can't eliminate your home or mobile phone, ask the provider about rates on other plans or any special deals that may be available. Do the same with all your insurance coverage. If you're not going to drop cable TV, get on the horn and see if you're eligible for that new advertised plan they're peddling. If they say it's just for new customers, *bitch* and see what happens. See what we're saying? Work to winnow those costs down. Then, when you cancel or reduce those bills, send the money you would have sent to those bills each month to your credit-card account. While it would be great if your landlord or mortgage company suddenly dropped two hundred dollars off your monthly payment, it's unlikely. However, most folks can cut *at least* this much off their fixed expenses. That's $2,400 a year. A good way to assess your fixed-cost flexibility is to print out a pie chart of your spending (see chapter 7). Work your way through every slice of the pie and think critically.

Example: You have a ninety-dollar-a-month gym membership. Ask yourself:

- How often do you go?
- How much is each visit costing you? (Twice a week means each visit costs you $11.25.)
- Are you only using the treadmill? Can't you walk in your neighborhood?
- If you're a yoga fan, couldn't you do yoga in your living room while watching a one-time-purchased tape?
- Could you replace any of your regular gym activities with a *free*, healthy, fun activity? Remember that friend you never seem to have time to see? Why not make a schedule to go on a (free) walk together on a regular basis?

CUT BACK ON DISCRETIONARY SPENDING

This is the big one. We already shared a few ideas for lopping this spending category in chapter 7. But it's worth saying here that this is where the most *choices* are being made in your budget. *You* decide when, where, and how often you'll eat out, for instance. No one's forcing you to go to the movies or to sporting events. *You* choose, just as you do when you shop for groceries, clothes, and home furnishings. If you can simply choose more carefully, you will (a) cease slapping more debt on your credit cards and (b) free up more money that can pay down those cards.

If you decide to stop indulging your happy-hour ritual, for example, send what you would have spent on your five afternoons of debauchery and lampshade headgear to your credit cards every Friday. If relatives slip you cash on birthdays or holidays, instead of blowing it like you normally do, send it in. With online payments these days, there's no reason to wait until the end of the billing cycle anymore. Log on and send. Did you earn points with all those credit-card charges? Instead of turning them into a plane ticket, convert them into cash, if you can, and send the windfall straight to your credit card. And on and on. Now, if this sounds like you won't have a life, guess what? You don't really have one now. That's the deal with debt. It robs you of money and time.

OTHER WAYS TO GET MONEY

A few other possibilities exist, but we think you should tread carefully here.

- If you have an existing retirement account, such as an old 401(k) or Roth, you may be tempted to borrow from or withdraw funds from the accounts to pay off your debts. Though this is legal to do, it's a bad idea, since you will jeopardize your investments' earning potential by raiding them. Let them do what they were designed to do—earn you money—and focus on paying down those cards with fresh incoming funds or trimmed expenditures.
- Borrowing money against your home—in the form of a home equity line of credit (HELOC) or a cash-out refinance—is sometimes recommended as a way of paying down credit cards. The idea is that you will be trading the high credit-card interest for a relatively lower interest rate on a loan. (Home loans are low interest because they're secured by the home.) Personally, we don't like mixing

bad with good debt. If you don't pay your credit-card bill, you end up with bad credit. If you fall behind on your bloated mortgage, you could lose your home.

- Transferring your balance to a lower-interest credit card can make sense if you understand what you're getting into. Zero-interest cards are tempting, but these offers are merely for an introductory period. Once the intro ends, the fee gets jacked to whatever the normal rate is. Low-interest-rate credit cards are more palatable, but a "promise" from a card issuer that it won't raise the rates is like getting Beelzebub to swear he'll stop stealing souls. In general, avoid cards that carry expensive transfer fees. If you must go this route, look for cards that cap the fee at a manageable level. Whatever you do, don't mistake this new relationship for friendship. They will still stick it to you in the form of higher rates if you are delinquent on your payments. And you must still commit to making more substantial payments on your cards until you get rid of them. Otherwise you are just borrowing from Peter to pay Paul, and they will both hike up their interest rates eventually.

GET RID OF THE CARDS—SLOWLY

OK. So you're squeezing some cash from your fixed monthly costs, discretionary spending, and Holy Trinity. Every time a check comes in the door, like clockwork, you are sending a percentage, *plus* any money you can scrounge up, to the credit card at the top of your list. Each time you do this, you are taking time to savor your dwindling balance. With each payment you make, your finance charges drop. That means more of your available income is going toward eradicating your principal debt.

As you pay off each card, cut it in half and tape both

halves to its designated manila folder in your file cabinet. You should always keep old card statements and the physical cards themselves as part of your paper—er, plastic trail. You may be tempted to phone the company and cancel the card once you've expunged the debt. Resist. Remember that your credit rating is linked to the amount of total credit you supposedly have. Cancel a card and your overall credit line will drop, meaning your credit scores will take a hit. The only cards you should *consider* canceling are the ones for which you are paying an annual fee. Cancel ones with the lowest credit line first, and drop only one per year. This way, it won't look like you lost access to a huge reservoir of credit all at once. You may have to pay an annual fee while you're waiting to drop a card, but it's small potatoes, considering what you've just been through. Don't bother canceling the non–annual fee cards. Should you keep and use any cards? We'll address this later. For now, focus on paying them off and cutting them up.

DONE? ASSESS WHAT YOU'VE LEARNED

We know this sounds daunting, and 10 percent may sound ridiculous. But it is a goal worth striving toward, even if you can't reach it initially. When J. D. Roth finished paying off his debt, he realized that for 3¼ years, he'd managed to scrape up about nine hundred to a thousand dollars a month to send to his cards. If he had that much money to play with, he figured, why couldn't he start saving it instead? And so he embarked on an ambitious plan to build an Emergency Account of twenty thousand dollars. When we last spoke to him, he was more than halfway there.

When you've paid off your last debt, you may be struck with

a strange feeling. On one hand, you'd like to celebrate. On the other, you'd rather not spend the money. In the time it took you to pay off every last dime, something changed within you. Living strictly within your means, and then some, has taught you that you can have a decent, reasonable life without overextending yourself.

As the happy survivor of a self-imposed debt fast, you'll be able to call upon these reserves of self-control any time you want. To save money. To lose weight. To work out. We predict that you will forever have a better handle on your spending. You'll know exactly which categories are the big temptations for you. You'll have a realistic idea of the kinds of "emergencies" that are most likely to tempt you to reach for the cards again. You may also be inspired to set more aggressive earning or saving goals for yourself. This is all powerful stuff. But you now have a few important decisions to make.

PAY OFF GOOD DEBTS—OR BUILD SAVINGS?

If you've truly wiped out all your debts—or you're about to—you're at an excellent stage of your life to make full use of this book. Savor the fact that the tables have now turned. After years of shelling out interest to various scumbag institutions, you're ready to have them start paying *you*! Sweet, delicious choices are waiting to be made. Should you, for instance, tackle the "good" debt in your life? Should you go nuts and pay off your student loans, your car, your mortgage?

While it's admirable to want to pay off all of these debts early, we happen to think that freelancers must live with *some* good debt while pursuing secondary financial goals. Why? Because you simply must build your own safety net; you don't have an employer building one for you. Say, for example, that you are saving 10 percent or 15 percent of every check to your Retirement Account, but your total retirement savings are still pretty anemic. Why not commit to upping that percent of your Holy Trinity to 20 percent or even 25 percent before paying off your car or student loan? Or why not commit to amassing a truly substantial Emergency Account that will help ensure that you'll never end up on credit cards again?

How do you decide what to do? It all comes back to the percentages. Get out the list of good debts you made in chapter 3 and look them over. Just what kind of interest are you paying on that student loan, car, or mortgage? Chances are the interest rates are relatively low (under 6 percent). If so, understand that you might stand to *earn* more by investing the money you have been paying to your credit cards in the stock market, mutual funds, or other investment vehicle. In other words, when you make an extra payment to a 3.25 percent student loan, you are in effect "earning" 3.25 percent on your money. If, instead, you buy mutual funds, you stand a chance of earning 5 percent, 8 percent, or even 15 percent on that money over the long haul.

Why earn less when you can earn more?

If you've absorbed some of the lessons of this book, you may be sputtering, "But I'm a freelancer! It pays for me to have as low an overhead as possible! Shouldn't I get rid of these bills, too?"

You're right. And we're right, too.

The point is, the decisions you make on this subject will be strongly influenced by the kind of person you are. Some people feel better having as much debt out of their lives as possible. That's fine, but as an independent worker you also need a well-stocked Emergency Account. Still others fear that they won't have enough to retire on.

We caution you: you can't listen to your employed friends on this topic. They have a skewed view of reality. They don't know what it's like in the trenches. These are people who probably *should* be saving more for their retirement than they really are but still have an invisible regimen of enforced savings bubbling in the background. While they're sitting there at the bar telling you to pay off your used Geo Metro, they are effortlessly investing chunks of pretax income in the stock market. Why the hell shouldn't you?

You need to do the math and listen to yourself. You might want to use a prepayment versus investment calculator (such as Hugh's at www.hughchou.org/calc/prepay_v_invest.cgi) to help you make up your mind. We warn you: the math is often not so clear-cut. While you can usually predict how long it'll take you to pay off a good debt, it's often impossible to predict what a stock will do in the short term. That's why you'll want to augment your calculations with a good list of pros and cons, as shown in the following box.

GOOD DEBT PAY-DOWN

The question: Should I pay off my car?

I'm paying 5.6 percent interest on it.

I owe $11,085 on it.

On average, I've been paying $3,900 to my credit cards each year.

I have $2,147 in my Emergency Account.

I want $43,200.

I have ____$22,000___ in all of my retirement funds.
I want _____much, much_____ more.

Pros:

- Paying off the car early will free up $230 a month. After I pay off the car, I can pay this extra $230 to the Emergency Account in addition to my standard percentage.
- I hate paying that car bill. Hate it, hate it.
- If I take what I was paying to the credit card and put it toward the car, I could pay off the car in twenty-one months, instead of fifty-four.

Cons:

- I get a tax deduction every year on those car payments because I use the car for my freelance business.
- I could split all the money I've been sending to my credit cards between my Emergency and Retirement accounts. If I did that, I'd save $3,900 extra this year alone.
- In the long term, I'd earn a higher rate of return (8 percent or more) on the portion I send to the Retirement Account. In the short term, I'd probably lose money.

This is not always a clear-cut decision. It will probably come down to your gut. We think it's worth doing the exercise to get it all down on paper. We personally would probably save more toward the Emergency Account and the Retirement Account.

But we don't want to sound like your mother.

SHOULD YOU GET A CREDIT CARD?

After all the hard work you've done, should you really get in bed with credit-card companies again? That depends. Some advisers hate credit cards so much that they strictly prohibit their clients, fans, readers, or adherents from ever touching one again. If you think you have a spending problem that's just itching to get back into the game, you may need to heed this advice. Otherwise, having at least one card seems practical for independent workers, especially if you travel or need to purchase goods and services for your business or clients. Assuming you will invoice your clients for these expenses or be reimbursed by the income you're earning, then a business bank account and accompanying business credit card makes sense. For personal use only, you may want to explore getting a charge card, one that requires payment in full every month. Either way, this time around, take your time to find the right card. Some tips:

- If you expect to run a balance—*for your business only!*—look for low rates. If you never plan to carry a balance ever again, choose a card with no annual fees, since the rates won't matter.

- Always remember and don't ever forget: the card companies make the rules and can change them at any time. Low introductory rates, zero-interest-for-a-year cards, and credit-card checks are all come-ons designed to snare you into spending beyond your means.

- Stay current on *all* your bills. Don't give them a chance to jack your rates up to 29.9 percent.

- The next time a sales clerk offers to take 10 percent off your current purchase if you open a store credit-card account, mock him or her mercilessly.

STAYING PUMPED

It's easy to get down on yourself when you're struggling to pay off debt. It's important to remember that the steps you are taking to dig yourself out are an empowering form of *action.* Many people simply resign themselves to a cycle of revolving debt. They take the sisyphean route, in other words. They cling to a kind of denial that somehow feels better than facing the enormous task head on.

Not you. Each dollar you pay off buys you freedom. You are inching your way toward the day when you begin funding your bigger goals. Because that's what all of this is about, anyway. *You deserve to be debt free.* You deserve to have the interest pendulum swing in your favor, now and forever. You deserve to invest in the power of your dreams.

WHAT TO DO

Debt is an icky subject, we know. But hey—doesn't it feel just a little bit good to finally be dealing with it? Do the following to make sure your new habits begin to stick.

- Examine the credit-card information you gathered in chapter 3. Choose which card you will pay down first and see if you can pay 10 percent of the total amount due to that card. If you can't, then work through each of the other options offered in this chapter. (p. 215)

- Plug your current debts and interest rates into an online credit-card calculator (like this one at Bankrate .com: www.bankrate.com/brm/calc/MinPayment.asp). Marvel at the effect that paying just a little bit more to your cards can have on the total amount of interest you pay and the time it takes to pay them off.

- Look at the Holy Trinity and devise a way to shift some of those percentages around—temporarily—in order to pay down your credit cards. (p. 217)

- Examine your fixed and discretionary costs (pp. 219–20). Find at least two categories where you could be shifting money to your credit-card payments.

PART III

GROWING THE PLAN AND LIVING THE DREAM

Money is only a tool.
It will take you wherever you wish,
but it will not replace you as the driver.

—**AYN RAND**

Now comes the good part: you're going to build on the basics and adapt the system to your burgeoning finances. With the skills you've gained, your dreams are within reach.

CHAPTER 10

GROWING THE SYSTEM

One of the most exciting and surprising things that we noticed when we started getting into this system was how psyched we began to feel about actually saving money. We still loved spending—who doesn't?—but the idea of saving became much more enthralling to us. We couldn't believe how simple it was. Even though we were saving just a little at a time, there was a method to it, a plan. We were involved, in control, well aware of what we were putting aside and, perhaps more important, why.

While it was still a little tough at first, because we were recovering from such steep financial losses, every time we saw the numbers in our savings accounts rise even just a little, it was incredibly rewarding. We looked forward to the next time that we were going to raise our percentages and were constantly evaluating our earning and spending in order to do so. It also became obvious that not only was this system working now . . . but it would continue to work. It was clearly adaptable to any earning or spending trends taking place in our lives. We also saw how it could easily and effortlessly help us save for other goals besides emergencies and taxes. Being able to do that, to save for specifics while still covering our necessities, helped us to get over a sometimes paralyzing and overly cautious thought pattern: *We can't put this money aside for a vacation—we might need it! Something could go terribly wrong!* But because we were already putting cash aside in the Emergency Account to take care of any horrible, unforeseen events that we were obsessing about, we didn't feel bad about putting some money aside for things we wanted, as well.

TIME TO GROW

In this chapter we are going to show you how to take your new savings savvy to the next level. As you and your career grow, your priorities will shift. Not to worry—this system can evolve right along with you. The system works because it easily adapts to the smallest incomes and then can seamlessly expand and grow along with your increased earnings. It works whether you're making $25,000 a year or $250,000 a year. It works if you're working part time, full time, or all the time. The power lies in percentages and habit building. As an independent worker, what really matters most is taking charge of your situation. Hopping in the driver's seat of that Maserati we talked about earlier, putting your foot on the gas, and running down anyone or anything that gets in the way of your savings goals. Eventually, you will experience the kind of attitude adjustment that your parents merely dreamed about for you. As each check comes in, your balances will grow and your wealth and confidence will increase. You will consider raising the percentages you have assigned to your savings goals. You, too, will become excited about saving.

As you reach savings goals and tackle debt, you will want to shift your savings focus to other categories. It couldn't be easier. This system can adjust to events in your life, whether or not you saw them coming. If your income increases markedly, the fact that you're using percentages ensures that you are setting enough aside to make up for that boon in bucks. You can constantly adjust your percentages and tailor your savings plan to fit what is going on in your life right now and continue to do so in the future. You will also be able to use the habits you've formed and the inherent flexibility of the system to save for key items and events in your life, not just bills and taxes. All of the work that you did in chapter 4 to help you identify the real financial priorities in your life will guide you as your savings priorities evolve and change over time. You will always be on target and focused on what really matters to you.

A CLOSER LOOK AT SCALABILITY

Let's take a more detailed look at how savings can grow along with your income, and how you can adjust your savings goals to remain in line with the financial priorities and needs you are experiencing right now and those you anticipate in your future.

For example: Let's say that you are currently saving 30 percent of your income of approximately thirty-eight thousand dollars per year. Then, oh joy oh joy, you land a new set of repeat clients. Your income rises by about twenty thousand dollars. Here's a look at how your yearly savings would automatically adjust to your new income level without your having to lift one pretty little finger.

ACCOUNTS	CURRENT INCOME $38,000	INCREASED INCOME $58,000
Emergency	5% = $1,900	5% = $2,900
Taxes	15% = $5,700	15% = $8,700
Retirement	10% = $3,800	10% = $5,800

AN EVEN CLOSER LOOK

You see? While the amount you have saved has gone up, the percentages you assigned have stayed the same. This is what makes saving with percentages so powerful: your savings adjust right along with the size of the checks, be they bigger or smaller.

You'll notice that the minimum amount we have you saving here is 30 percent. This really is a minimum you want to keep in mind if you are solely responsible for all of your taxes, all of your retirement, and your emergencies. As you can see, the savings really begin to add up once you get into the more significant percentages. Don't assume that you can't do this. Most people, as we've said before, can squeeze a lot more out of their income than they think they can. If your goals and priorities are clear and you've experienced the joy of seeing your financial picture improve just a little bit, you will become anxious to make saving even more of a priority. A spike in income is the prime opportunity to ramp up your savings.

Look again at the numbers in the chart. If you add up the total savings in each column and subtract that number from the income to which it applies, you will notice the following: For the $38,000 income, the amount of money left over and available for your fixed and discretionary costs after you set aside money for savings is $26,600. Keeping to the same percentages, but at the increased income of $58,000, the amount of money you have left over after savings that can be spent on your fixed and discretionary costs is $40,600. That's quite a boost. "Let's go shopping!" you say. Don't do it. Fight the urge. Get yourself a little something nice or take yourself out for a celebratory dinner, but remember this: what you are really celebrating is the fact that if you do not increase your fixed monthly costs and keep your discretionary spending right where it is, you are now in the prime position to seriously up your savings percentages.

For example:

ACCOUNTS	CURRENT INCOME $38,000	INCREASED INCOME $58,000
Emergency	5% = $1,900	15% = $8,700
Taxes	15% = $5,700	20% = $11,600
Retirement	10% = $3,800	15% = $8,700
Money available to you after savings	**$26,600**	**$29,000**

Well, would you lookee there. . . . You upped your total savings percentage to a whopping 50 percent, and you *still* have more money to put toward your fixed and discretionary costs. In fact, you have $2,400 more each year, which works out to be about $200 each month. That could go a long way to saving for a dream goal, perhaps one that you outlined in chapter 4. (If you want to see even more ideas for saving, check out the box on pages 250–51.)

Having a goal of setting aside at least 40 percent or even 50 percent of your income to divide among your various accounts is not unreasonable. Remember: being an independent worker means you have to save more, plain and simple.

WHEN IS THE RIGHT TIME TO UP OR ADJUST YOUR PERCENTAGES?

Whenever you feel ready. Seriously, once you get into the savings groove you will be excited to do this. Jacking up your percentages after an increase in income, like the one we showed above, is only one example of a reason to amplify your savings—although it happens to be an awfully good one.

You should constantly be monitoring your income. (Come on—as a freelancer you're probably doing that anyway.) And you should be on the lookout for opportunities to increase and focus your savings to get the most mileage out of the efforts you are so diligently making toward revamping your Spending Identity.

ASSESSING AT TAX TIME

You must not only keep a watchful eye on your earning and spending trends while seeking to pounce mercilessly on just the right time to adjust what you're socking away. You must also make an effort to give your life a full financial once-over on a regular basis. Taking stock of your finances and filling in the dots in your fiscal color-by-numbers as you worked through this book is one thing. And congratulations on taking the time and having the gumption to do it. But no two years are the same in a freelancer's life. Trends occur, new spending comes into play, priorities shift. You must commit to routinely reassessing your income and spending and goals so that you are sure you are staying on track. We humbly suggest that you take advantage of what is normally considered by society to be a stressful, depressing season—tax season—and use it instead to get pumped about a whole new year of saving for and attaining goals.

As you prepare to send in your final numbers for the year to your tax guru, take note of your profile for the past year:

- How much did you earn?

- How much did you save?
- How much did you spend on your discretionary costs as a whole?
- Now look at categories that you know give you trouble (eating out, maybe). How did you do this year?
- Did your debt go up or down?

Based on the answers to the above questions, you may want to make some adjustments. For example: If your debt went up, you may want to shift percentages to take care of it. If your discretionary spending was a bit out of hand, you know you have room in your accounts to save even more.

Another thing you can do is the following simple calculation.

1. Take the gross amount that you earned.
2. Subtract the amount that you saved (for retirement, emergencies, everything).
3. Subtract the amount you paid in taxes.

Your answer represents the amount of money you had for your fixed and discretionary spending. So now . . .

4. Multiply your fixed monthly costs by twelve.
5. Now subtract the new number from the number you got in step 3 above.

This answer represents the amount of money you had available to you for discretionary spending throughout the year. Is it more or less than you thought? Is it time to save more? Do you think you can bank on the same earnings this year?

Again, if you know your fixed monthly costs and what you've made over the years, you can very easily see how much room you have for saving and how your overhead is working with your current earnings.

Another fun thing to do (OK, not crazy, make-a-margarita-in-your-mouth fun, but fun nonetheless) is to look at the amount that you calculated you would have left over for discretionary spending and start playing with an online wealth calculator.

For example: Say you look at your available cash for discretionary spending from last year and the number was much higher than you anticipated. You wonder what would happen if you committed to putting another fifteen thousand dollars away each year in a taxable account (a brokerage account, for example). Let's even assume that your income never goes up. How much will that fifteen thousand dollars turn into in twenty-five years if you get the average 8 percent return over time? **$952,623.** Yeah, baby! Doesn't that get you psyched? The miracle of compound interest strikes again.

So take time on a regular basis to examine your finances and think long and hard about your future: What is your goal? To live on 50 percent of your income? Could you live on 40 percent? How frugal can you be and still feel rich because you're taking steps to invest in your dreams?

MAKING ADJUSTMENTS: SOME COMMON SCENARIOS

In addition to a rise in income, here are some other situations that are opportunities to assess how much of a percentage you are saving and what you're directing your savings toward:

- **YOU HAVE REDUCED YOUR FIXED MONTHLY COSTS.** Sometimes people—us included—decide to reduce their overhead as a means of freeing up money. We decided to move away from an expensive city. For us, that meant our work and earning life became more relaxed. With reduced overhead, we had more flexibility to get our finances in shape.

- **YOU NOTICE THAT YOUR MONEY IS GOING FURTHER THAN IT USUALLY DOES.** Month after month, you are noticing that you have a nice cushion in your Spending Account and you almost never need to dip into your Emergency Account. Fantastic! Now you are in the perfect position to up your percentages and save even more. Chances are, you won't feel a thing.

- **YOU HAVE A FINANCIAL GOAL THAT MEANS A LOT TO YOU,** and you are willing to reduce your discretionary spending in order to save more. Sometimes the decision to increase your percentages is based simply on the will and desire to achieve a financial goal that is important to you. That's all the motivation you need, and if you are that passionate and committed, you will succeed. Hike up those savings!

- **YOU HAVE FINISHED PAYING OFF A MAJOR DEBT.** Oh, what a glorious feeling! To see a debt eradicated is better than [insert naughty pleasure here]. Now don't change a thing! Keep setting aside the same amount of money you were for that debt, but direct it to something that means a lot to you.

- **YOUR EMERGENCY ACCOUNT IS MAXED OUT.** The great thing about the Emergency Account is that it's finite.

Unlike taxes and retirement, which you will be contributing to for a very, very long time, once you've maxed out the Emergency Account you can shift that percentage to other goals.

- **THE MAJORITY OF YOUR INCOME IS ALREADY TAXED.** If you've recently increased your hours as a part-time worker, independent contractor, or permalancer and have taxes taken out of your paycheck already, you do not need to save for taxes as aggressively as many other independent workers. If you commit to saving a sizable portion of your pay that would have previously gone to your tax account, you can achieve some major financial goals in a short amount of time.

So now what? If you noticed you have the ability to save more, have recently paid off a debt, or simply are willing to really cut back in order to achieve a particular financial goal, here are some suggestions of ways you can take your savings to the next level. These are at your discretion, of course. Many people decide that rather than save for something new, they just want to save much more for retirement. That's a fine option. The important thing is to consciously decide where you want your money to go and then put it there.

THE HEALTH ACCOUNT

Every day, it seems more likely that a national solution to the health-care problem will be implemented. Why? Because more than forty-six million people in the United States are currently living without health insurance. And—big surprise—the number is growing. But you simply can't hold your breath waiting for that day. If you've established a healthy Emergency Account, you may choose to add a Health Account. You would select a new percentage and begin diverting that amount from every paycheck to the new account.

You would use this account to

- save for monthly or quarterly insurance premiums;
- save for upcoming health-care costs;
- sock away money that will ultimately be sent to a Health Savings Account (HSA). (More about HSAs on p. 245.)

This is one of the largest and most annoying expenses for the self-employed. Individual plans—even the "emergency" coverage that only seems to pay if you're already dead—are insanely expensive, and individuals and small business owners often do not benefit from group rates. If you are married and your spouse has health-care coverage through a traditional employer, congratulations. You really lucked out in the marriage lottery. In fact, if you're a single, independent worker, don't even think of marrying another independent worker. Marry only for health care.

We're trying to be funny here, but health insurance is no joke. It's easy for a twentysomething freelancer to get the impression that he or she will never get sick. But this is tempting fate. Don't flirt with disaster. Take whatever steps are necessary to get health care. Investigate professional organizations, unions, or guilds in your line of work that offer group insurance at group rates. Joining such a group may necessitate paying an annual membership fee, but this is a small price to pay for decent coverage at a good rate. Organizations such as the National Association for the Self-Employed (www.nase .org) and the Freelancers Union (www.freelancersunion.org) cater specifically to independent workers. Barring this, check out private health insurance rates at eHealthInsurance (www .ehealthinsurance.com).

Brace yourself for sticker shock as you shop for health insurance. Insurance companies can jack up their rates every year—or nearly so—and it often feels as if they are bilking the poor independent worker to offset losses they may be experiencing in the traditional work world. There's no way around the high costs. If it's any consolation, the cost of health care is *fully tax deductible* for self-employed people. Make sure your tax preparer takes these deductions on your behalf:

- You can take a self-employed health insurance deduction, which allows you to deduct medical and dental insurance premiums every year. (Look for line 29 on your 1040 tax form.)
- You can deduct all contributions to an HSA, just as you would contributions to an IRA account. (See line 25 on the ol' 1040.)

If you still think you absolutely cannot afford health insurance, at the very least look into a High-Deductible Health Plan (HDHP) that would cover you in the case of a major medical disaster. Premiums are lower—or at least are supposed to be—but doctor visits for a random sore throat or routine physicals would totally be on you. If you participate in an honest-to-goodness HDHP, you're allowed to save extra money for medical expenses in a tax-deductible account called a health savings account (HSA). HSAs are relatively new; President George W. Bush signed these accounts into law in 2003. Most health-insurance companies let you establish an HSA with them, but you may also have the option to open an account with a financial firm, such as Vanguard. You cannot use the money in the HSA to pay your premiums, just your medical expenses. It's a great way to save up for things you know you will need, such as dental surgery, hospital stays, prescription eye care, or elective treatments.

Any deposits you make to an HSA reduce your taxable income for that year and grow tax free. Unlike a flex spending account from an employer, these balances roll over from one year to the next. (The 2010 maximum deposits were $3,050 for singles and $6,150 for families.) If you take the money out for nonmedical reasons, you must pay a 10 percent penalty. The accounts do have their critics, who say HSAs are simply a Band-Aid on a growing national problem. Only you and your spouse (if applicable) can decide if it makes sense for you to use an HDHP. Your tax preparer will be able to advise you, based on an analysis of your past health-care costs.

Kathleen Campbell, the financial planner from Florida whom you met in chapter 6, participates in an HDHP herself, since she's self-employed and rarely needs to go to the doctor. But she did spend a little extra money getting a more traditional health plan with all the jimmies for her seven-year-old daughter, because a kid will always get into crazy scrapes. "I didn't want to be in the position of asking myself, 'Hmm, do I really want to pay for this doctor's visit out of pocket?' " she says, explaining her choice. Now her daughter can go to the doctor anytime, and Mom just makes a co-payment.

IMPORTANT DOCUMENTS EVERYONE NEEDS

Along with health insurance, every independent worker needs a few other important documents to round out his or her just-in-case portfolio. We'd love to spell out exactly what *you*, dear reader, need, but alas, you should really consult with a financial planner and attorney to decide what's right for you. Here are the highlights.

INSURANCE

Life insurance: Most people shrug off life insurance because they don't think they need it. "I'll get it when I'm hitched," they say, then complain ten years later that plans are ridiculously unaffordable. Think ahead: Yes, if you have a spouse, kids, future college payments, and a mortgage, you absolutely need life insurance. And if you're a single, twenty- or thirty-something freelancer, it might pay to *consider* life insurance when you're still young, fit as a fiddle, and able to lock in a dirt-cheap premium. Likewise, if you're partners in a small business with a buddy of yours, it pays to get life insurance to protect each other in case one of you takes the Big Sleep. You don't want to be stuck paying massive company loans on business property or equipment, for example. For our money, *term life insurance*—the kind where you pay a fixed premium for protection across a fixed period of time such as ten, twenty, or thirty years—is best. Avoid pushy insurance salespeople who work on commission. Consult first with a good financial planner or attorney.

Disability insurance: This is the independent worker's version of workers' comp. Disability is actually more important than life insurance for younger people (under fifty). That's because they're more likely to become disabled in a rock-climbing accident than they are to kick the bucket. If you can't work for months at a time, how will you cover your expenses? An employed person will usually have disability coverage as part of their benefits package, but what about you?

YOUR ESTATE

An estate plan: We can hear the "estate-less" among you guffawing already. But you can still die or become incapacitated, and you probably don't want some judge deciding what will happen to your possessions, or, heaven forbid, your own bad self. A good estate plan should include all or some of the following items.

- ***A revocable living trust with an incapacity clause:*** A revocable trust is a document used to set up a trustee (or "fiduciary") to hold and manage your assets. Normally, *you* are the trustee, until such time as you cannot manage your own assets. Basically, a trust runs like a kind of mini family corporation. If you die, the trust survives and simply passes management of its assets along to the next trustee. People like trusts because they keep family affairs private and avoid what can be costly probate proceedings. "People don't ask their lawyers for trusts because they think they're expensive and they're only for rich people," a financial planner told us. "But they're not. My parents are blue-collar folks with not a lot of money, and they have a trust."

- ***A will:*** Even if you have a trust, you will probably still want a will. Why? There may be assets you forgot to put in the trust, or those that are paid to your estate *after* your death. Also, we tend to forget the little things. A will may be the best way to make sure your kid sister inherits your killer costume jewelry collection. Otherwise, all those wonderful pieces might end up at a white elephant sale, going for a buck-fifty a pop.

- ***A durable power of attorney for health care and advance directives (aka living will):*** In the event you are incapacitated, these documents will give your friends or family the legal right to consult with doctors, pay medical bills, and make critical health-care decisions on your behalf. Some states require a living will to be a separate document.

Listen up: these documents are too important to risk creating them on your own using books, online programs, or flashy but outdated software. There's too much at stake. Laws and terminology vary from state to state, and an amateur can easily create an invalid document or one that will create bigger problems down the line for family members. Only a reputable local attorney should advise you as to which papers you'll need based on your specific situation.

We *get* the aversion to hiring a lawyer. We do. They look scary on TV, what with the fancy suits and the constant objecting in court. But in real life, most are quite approachable schlubs in rumpled clothing. The total cost for estate documents should not be more than one thousand to two thousand dollars. That's not a lot of money for thoroughly legal peace of mind.

THE DREAM ACCOUNTS

Up to this point, the accounts we've discussed have been for things that you *must* take care of—emergencies, taxes, retirement, health care. Now, at long last, we turn to the real reason you and everyone on earth toils: to fund our dreams.

About freaking time, you're thinking, and you absolutely have a point. Dreams are the things that make life worth living, but we would argue that your life is in peril if you don't take care of the other essentials first.

What good is a scuba trip in the Caribbean if you don't have health care to cover you when you get the bends?

How will that Mini Cooper help you pay Uncle Sam?

How will the kayak, the camera, and all those other desires you listed back in chapter 4 help you in times of income interruption?

That's why we've waited until now. You simply must build the fundamentals into your saving structure and pay off serious debt before contemplating expendable, but still quite important, objects of desire.

Adding one or more dream accounts to your growing list of online saving accounts marks a significant priority shift. It means you are

- openly stating what you want;
- shunning credit cards in favor of patiently saving;
- willing to make the item a part of your growing financial profile.

Notice we call these Dream Account*s*. Plural. None of us has one single dream, so it makes sense to establish as many accounts as you need. Is there a limit? Not really, but we would advise that you stick to no more than one or two accounts to start. As you get more experience, as you reduce your overhead, as you get smarter with money, you will be able to add more accounts and devote a greater percentage of your earnings toward your dreams.

For now, pick one or two high-ranking dreams from the list you created in chapter 4. Establish online accounts for these dreams and name them well. Be specific. Choose joyful names. It's nice to see the name of your dream staring back at you every time you visit your accounts and watch them swell with monthly interest.

A SAMPLING OF NAMES FOR DREAM ACCOUNTS

Zoe's College Account

My Scuba Account

Our Caribbean Beach Vacation Account

The Blue Lexus Account

My Fight Homelessness Account

Christmas/Hanukkah Account

Great Outdoors Account

- Addition to the House Account
- Replacing Drafty Windows Account
- Family Reunion 2015 Account
- New iMac Computer Account
- Pottery Kiln Account
- Dave's Stamp Collecting Fund
- Linda's Sewing/Knitting Account
- House Painting Account
- Experience Fabulous New Wines Account
- Cabin in the Woods Account
- Walter's Orthodonture Account
- Condo Down Payment Account
- Mom & Dad's Surprise 60th Anniversary Account
- Spiritual Journey to Tibet Account
- Car Maintenance Account
- New Kitchen Account
- Wedding Account
- Honeymoon Account

If you look at the box above, you'll see that these are all admirable Dream Accounts. They are hobby dreams, vacation dreams, outrageous material possession dreams, charitable dreams, and family-related dreams. After you've chosen the dreams, named them, and opened the accounts, the next important step is to choose the percentages you will allocate on a per-check basis to each of these accounts. By now, you will be an old hand at this. Go ahead and choose percentages that are realistic and appropriate.

What do we mean? Simply this: vacations are lovely, but it's not appropriate to toss 20 percent of your pay at a Bahamas getaway and a mere 5 percent to a down payment on a home or a child's education. That's why we asked you to rank your dreams and goals back in chapter 4. If you've done this correctly, you should be able to assign appropriate percentages to your dreams. From there, it's a cakewalk to start funneling money to them as each paycheck comes in the door.

Let's take a look at how you might reprioritize your savings accounts.

In this scenario, we'll assume a saver . . .

- has been saving a total of 30 percent in her accounts;
- recently paid off a large credit-card debt;
- wants to save 40 percent or possibly more;
- wants to save for a few dreams.

Watch the evolution, left to right, as the debt is expunged and the Emergency Account is maxed, despite little or no change in income.

ACCOUNTS	DESIRED TOTAL PERCENTAGE: 30% (DEBTOR STYLE)	DESIRED TOTAL PERCENTAGE: 40% (DEBT-FREE)	DESIRED TOTAL PERCENTAGE: 45% (AFTER MAXING OUT EMERGENCY ACCOUNT)
Emergency	3%	10%	Maxed out! 0%
Taxes	15%	15%	15%
Retirement	5%	15%	20%
Credit cards	7%	0%! Hurray!	Still 0%! Yessss!
Health account	N/A	N/A	5%
Condo down payment	N/A	N/A	4%
My weekend photography trips	N/A	N/A	1%

From this example, you can see that the saver has made some conscientious decisions:

- She has committed to increasing her retirement percentage.
- She's socking away money for health-care costs.
- She's started saving for a condo and some weekend trips that are important to her.

Her total percentage—45 percent—is ambitious. But she believes her choices are realistic for her at this time. She values the condo more than her weekend trips, so they are being funded to reflect this. She'd love to save even more for her retirement, but she refuses to do this at the expense of her dreams, and there's no way she can bump her savings up to 50 percent of her income. Not at this time.

We don't blame her. For most people, saving 40 percent to 45 percent is about as high as they can go. You'd have to reduce your overhead drastically—assume the cheapest rent or mortgage possible, drive your used car forever, and live a remarkably frugal life—to save more beyond this. Don't get us wrong. *It* is *possible, and we encourage you to try it when the time is right for you.*

If you're wise enough to read between the lines, you can see that there are a lot of hard choices in these percentages. If our plucky saver earns a hundred thousand dollars a year, she'll sock away a thousand dollars by the end of the year for weekend photography trips. This isn't a heckuva lot, and she may well be tempted to slap her trips on her credit card. But she won't do this. She's sacrificed too much to live debt free. We admire her.

INVESTING YOUR DREAM MONEY

Your Dream Accounts, like your Retirement Account, are merely collection points on the way to greater earnings. You wouldn't want to leave the cash for an important long-term goal, such as a child's education or a house down payment, in a bank savings account earning minuscule interest. No, you'd invest it in a worthy financial instrument that would allow that money to grow until you needed it. In chapter 4, we talked about retirement funds keyed to your target date of retirement. Dream Accounts should also be invested according to how soon you'll need the money.

If you need the money in . . .

Under three years	Leave it in the bank savings account or put it in a certificate of deposit (CD).
Three to five years	Invest it in a low- to moderate-risk portfolio (20% stocks, 60% bonds, 20% cash reserves).
More than five years	Invest it somewhere between a moderate-risk (40% stocks, 60% bonds) and a high-risk portfolio (65% stocks, 35% bonds).
More than ten years	Invest it in a high-risk portfolio (65% to 90% stocks, 35% to 10% bonds).

A number of financial-services companies offer products tailored to this kind of investing. One firm will call them life strategy funds, another will call them goal-oriented funds, and still others dub them conservative, intermediate (or moderate), and growth funds. (We urge you to investigate the funds, questionnaires, and calculators offered by the financial firms in the appendix.) The important thing is to choose a mix of stocks, bonds, and cash that carries a level of risk you can live with. As we've said before, the longer you can wait to use the money, the greater risk you can assume.

Many people will want to keep the money right where it is, in their online bank savings account. We've noticed this interesting tendency: people have no problem investing and risking their retirement money, but they have trouble investing their dream money. Possibly, this is because their retirement seems a long way off, so distant that they can't imagine what that period of their life will be like. In contrast, dreams are deeply felt, closely held, and hard to risk. We want them *now.* And the stock market, regardless of when you're reading this, always seems like a huge risk.

We understand this. That's why we're making you set up the online savings accounts for these dreams. Above all, we want you to start saving for them. Next, we'd like you to take the time to educate yourself. In time, we'd love it if you came to realize that the best place for your child's college money is not in a bank account earning 2 percent but invested in an education savings plan (such as a 529 Plan) earning a higher percentage and offering tax advantages. When you're ready to take the plunge and invest for greater growth, the money will still be in your savings account, ready to be invested. Just don't wait too long.

For now, the chart on page 256 shows how we envision disbursing the money from a single check to all these different accounts. In this example, we're using the same 45 percent goal expressed in the chart on page 252. Remember, the Emergency Account has already been maxed out, so you won't see it here. Notice that only two accounts—the Retirement Account and the Condo Account—are being invested for long-term growth. (The saver doesn't expect to buy for another ten years.)

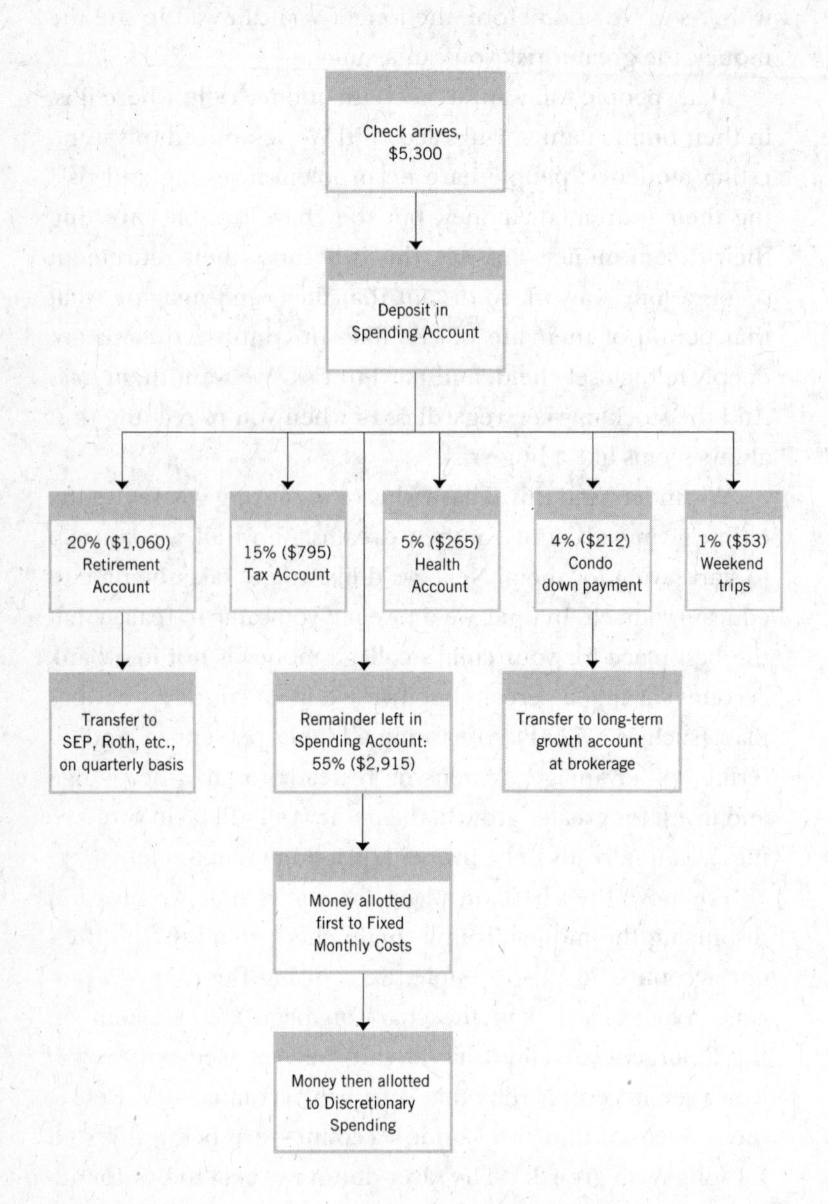
Check arrives,
$5,300
Deposit in
Spending Account
20% ($1,060)
Retirement
Account
15% ($795)
Tax Account
5% ($265)
Health
Account
4% ($212)
Condo
down payment
1% ($53)
Weekend
trips
Transfer to
SEP, Roth, etc.,
on quarterly basis
Remainder left in
Spending Account:
55% ($2,915)
Transfer to long-term
growth account
at brokerage
Money allotted
first to Fixed
Monthly Costs
Money then allotted
to Discretionary
Spending

WHAT ABOUT BUSINESS ACCOUNTS?

If you keep a business checking account separate from your personal accounts, we hope you'll consider setting up a similar trajectory to save for business goals as well. Yes, we know it's prudent to save for business taxes, emergencies such as not being able to pay rent on an office, business insurance, and so on. But regardless of your line of work, you may very well want new equipment, tools, or money to travel to an annual conference. Set up those accounts, too, and start funding them. Don't neglect your business dreams!

PURSUING YOUR DREAMS WHILE KEEPING DEBT UNDER CONTROL

Say, after all this, you make an overly spendy credit-card purchase without having the cash because you feel your business has to have a particular item. Or say you incurred some medical bills and now you have a sizable debt that you didn't have before.

How does this alter your best-laid plans? What happens to your percentages now?

First, don't panic. Sit down and crunch the numbers. Work down this algorithm of increasingly sacrificial choices:

1. If it's just one fixed bill, decide if you can afford to keep your current percentages unchanged while paying down the debt out of upcoming discretionary funds. If you

can, do that. This route is the least disruptive to your saving regimen.

2. If you can cover the debt out of your Emergency Account and save yourself the many months of credit-card interest, do this. But you must then commit to paying back the money you borrowed from yourself—either out of future discretionary funds or by suspending payments to Dream Accounts only.

3. If the amount you owe is too great, *retreat.* Fund only your Tax and Retirement Accounts while you divert the remainder of your percentages to your debt. Suspend funding of your Emergency (provided you have at least one month's worth of costs in there), Health, and Dream Accounts until the monster is slain.

If you find yourself consistently backsliding, try to assess what's gone wrong.

- Has your business undergone a fundamental shift?
- Do you need to work harder to attract clients or customers?
- Are you experiencing an exceptionally bad gap period where no pay is coming in?
- Have you suffered an unusual financial setback, such as an illness?

If they don't already know the answers to these questions, most savvy freelancers can usually track down the answer by running analyses of their income and expenses in their financial software programs.

Sometimes you are at fault. You expanded too quickly. You had a bad month of spending. You opted for the dream *now* versus the delayed dream.

Sometimes, nothing's really changed. The situation you're in feels all too familiar. You're living a feast-or-famine freelance life from which there seems to be no escape.

Other times, it's not you at all. Chances are, if your overhead or spending hasn't changed but your income has tanked, you may be in the grip of a major economic crisis that's larger than you.

Thankfully, in all three of these situations, the solution's the same: you can lower your overhead, rein in spending, and commit to earning more money. Which brings us to the next chapter.

WHAT TO DO

You've now taken it to the next level. You are saving beyond the necessary and have ventured into the land of dreams. Stay on track by doing the following:

- Think ahead: without looking back at your work from chapter 4, make a list of the next three things you would save for when you increase your percentages. Would you put more toward retirement, or is there something special you want to dedicate your cash to? Now compare this list to the priorities you named in chapter 4. How do they stack up?

- In addition to remaining vigilant about earning and spending patterns in your life, commit to formally evaluating your earnings and spending from the top down (the way you did in chapter 2) at least once per year, with an eye toward finding extra money to set aside for your dreams.

- Create a worst-case scenario game plan that you can rely on in the event of an unexpected financial upheaval—a substantial loss of income, a drastic increase in debt, and so on. Examine how you would adjust your percentages and your lifestyle to get your finances back on track. (pp. 257–59)

CHAPTER 11

BUILDING PROSPERITY

Over the years, we have come to notice the following: most people—at least those with two or more brain cells to rub together—don't go freelance for the money, but the majority of them abandon freelance life because of money. We have watched many remarkably talented colleagues hang up their self-employed spurs for the security of a full-time job. And we get it. While the allure of working for yourself is a powerful one, it also comes with a great deal of responsibility: responsibility to yourself to be completely frank about how things are going.

There are two people we know who we feel capture both the good and the not-so-good about the independent working life.

The first is Sarah, a former art director at a children's publishing company. Sarah decided to leave her job, a good, stable one at a very well-known outfit. She had the kind of job that others in her field would commit felonies in order to get. But she felt like she was in a rut. She wanted new challenges and the opportunity to work on her own projects. She wanted to meet other people in her field and feel more in control of her own work destiny, so to speak. So she left her job and set out for greener freelance pastures.

Some months after her departure, she was talking about what kept her at it, despite the unexpected twists and turns that she was still learning to maneuver. In short, what kept her fires stoked was the idea of unlimited potential. She liked the idea that she could wake up every morning with the feeling that this could be the "big day." She liked not being chained to a desk forever, working on the same projects with the same people. There was all of this potential lurking just in the distance, always the idea that she could "make it big," or become involved with a project that really inspired her and set her up financially. No one else was imposing any limits on her. She wasn't stuck with the same salary, no matter what.

Then there's Emily, another remarkable freelance friend of ours who worked for years as a brilliant researcher for institutions, television shows—you name it. Within the last year she decided she wanted—and she found—a full-time job. This came after years of very successful but exhausting and stressful work on her own. She took a job performing the exact same kind of duties that she did when she was working independently. The main difference was that she was now performing those duties for a law firm. We were absolutely thrilled for her when she found this job. Why? Because she is happy. And she's happy because (color us shocked) she will now have insurance (dental!), a 401(k), and all the other financially beneficial scootchies that go along with J-O-B-S.

We are happy for Sarah and Emily. They are both doing what works best for them. How did they arrive at that? They were honest with themselves. They assessed their situations and made informed choices based on their values and goals, much like the ones you set for yourself in chapter 4. And this is the message for this chapter: In order to be successful and prosperous you have to be honest with yourself. In order to effect change—and deciding to streamline your finances and take on new fiscal habits is a pretty major change—you have to take stock of who you are, what you want, and why you're doing what you're doing.

It may be that you've been following the system for a couple months but you're getting frustrated: You don't feel as though you're saving enough. You're still depending too much on your credit cards, and your attempts to pay them off are beginning to feel like a Sisyphean excursion up Mount Everest. You're dipping into the Emergency Account more than you'd like and having a hard time paying back what you owe yourself. So what can you do? There are really only three main actions you can take:

- earn more
- spend less
- lower your overhead

Now, don't get snippy—we can hear you: *If it were that easy I would have done it already*. Would you? We are going to look with you now at ways you can bring more prosperity into your life.

Again, not all independent workers are created equal. You may be a work-at-home illustrator, or you may be an actor by day and bartender by night. You may be working two part-time jobs, neither of which pays you what you deserve. You could be a permalancer with dreams of writing the great American novel. But whether or not you chose this lifestyle, it's the one that you have.

If you don't want to be freelance, moving from gig to giggity gig, but have to do so for now, examining how you work and how you earn can only help you land the job you really want. If you have chosen the independent working lifestyle and have pinned all of your hopes and dreams on making the freelance life work, your success absolutely depends on constantly assessing not only what you're making but how well you are doing your job. Here, we give you some starting points.

CLIENT RELATIONS

If you sell something, you have clients. If you offer a service, you have clients. If you create art, you have clients. In short, there has to be someone on the other end of a transaction who gives you money, whether that person is buying a product or a service from you. Who are these mysterious and sometimes elusive fish that we all strive to catch?

KNOW WHO'S BUTTERING YOUR BREAD

At least once a year—tax time is a good time to do this—you should take a good look at where your money is coming from. Is the majority of it coming from one or two major clients? If you're in sales, are there just a handful of customers who carry most of the ordering weight? And if you're working part time or temping, where is most of your money coming from? An agency? Your own efforts? Once you've identified those who are bringing you the most money and those who are lingering around the periphery of your breadwinning circle, you will want to do a couple of things.

First, evaluate how well you are servicing those clients or customers who consistently come through for you. Are you taking their contributions for granted? Think of a way to reach out to them and let them know you value their business. A simple card or letter, a short phone call—these can all provide you with opportunities to explore how you might serve them better. Don't be afraid to ask—the answer might mean increased revenue for you.

Then look at those folks who are in the second tier of payment. Do any of these people have the potential to become more regular clients? Reach out to those who do. And remember: be confident and friendly, not desperate and needy.

LOOK FOR NEW BUTTER

Independent workers should always be on the lookout for new job opportunities, new inroads to clients, new ways to expand what they're doing.

- **MARKETING.** Do not be afraid to toot your own horn. In fact, make it a bullhorn. If you need a Web site, put one up. If you can't afford a swanky Web designer, then use a cheap—but clean and professional-looking—template while saving for an upgrade. If you really want to make a big marketing push, via print, Web, TV, or radio, find out how much it will cost and then, if you can't afford it now, make it a goal. Start setting aside a percentage of your income to make it happen.
- **NETWORKING.** Truth be told, a lot of people who work from home really enjoy the fact that they don't have to interact with a bunch of other people every day. But here's the deal: sometimes you have just got to take a bullet for the biz. Get out of the home office, take that long-overdue shower, put on some clean clothes, and move beyond your misanthropic tendencies. You never know whom you might meet. Get involved with freelancing groups, many of which host mixers where people can

swap stories—and sometimes job contacts. Look into a Toastmasters group near you to bring you out of your shell and meet other people. Get involved with your guild or union and attend meetings. Reach out (come on, you can do it, it won't hurt) to someone in your field with whom you feel comfortable. Have a coffee, swap war stories and techniques. And if it floats your boat, find a mentor. Approach someone who has been doing what you're doing a lot longer than you have—and ideally with a great deal of success—and offer to buy them lunch. Be upfront about the fact that you would like to pick their brain about how they run their business. Most individuals—except for the freakishly paranoid—will take this as a major compliment and will happily oblige.

ALWAYS BE PROFESSIONAL

This may sound like obvious advice, but not everyone takes it to heart—especially when things aren't going exactly as they'd hoped. Any independent worker who depends on clients for their business must be religiously professional, no matter the circumstances, because their return business and their reputation depend on it. Does that mean that you must silently tolerate rude and inappropriate clients? Not at all. What it *does* mean is that if you have an issue with one of your clients or are simply dealing with someone who is a bit testy, there is a right way and a wrong way to handle things.

So what do you do if you're frustrated with a client? A lot of it depends on whether or not you ever want to work with that person again and whether or not they are in a position to refer you to others. If the answer is no to both of these, and you are positive that you have completed the work to the best of your abilities—and made any requested changes—then simply thank them for the opportunity to work with them. And never accept work from them ever again. Let them wonder why. If you still have unresolved issues regarding the work you were contracted to do, work to focus the energy on resolving those issues as efficiently as possible and politely remind them that, though you appreciate their frustration, things will get done more quickly and economically if all parties refrain from anger and stay focused on the task at hand. It is almost never worth exploding back at someone who has treated you disrespectfully. It is always better to take the high road, keep the project on target, and quietly resolve never to work with the person again.

If you do want to work with them again and do not appreciate the manner in which they are treating you, the same tactic usually works. If criticism is given, address it head-on. If someone treats you with what you consider to be disrespect, point it out to them in a direct yet professional manner. And do so under the guise of putting personalities aside for the sake of the project. If someone has been particularly obscene, it is fine to tell them that you do not appreciate their unprofessional manner and that if they want this project to be the best it can be, it is in everyone's best interest to remain focused on the task at hand and work wisely, not angrily. Another really fun perk of taking the high road is that it almost *always* frustrates and perplexes the hell out of someone who has no self-control. They rarely know how to respond.

The longer you work, the better you will become at being able to spot trouble clients at a distance and avoid working with them at all. Until then, remain the consummate pro, even when they try to drag you down into the gutter.

DON'T BE AFRAID OF THE "M" WORD

One of the keys to earning what you need is asking for what you deserve. Do research, of course, and make sure that your rates fall within the industry standard. And if you are someone with limited experience living in a small city, make sure you aren't asking for rates that a seasoned pro would demand in a major metropolis.

PRACTICE ASKING FOR WHAT YOU DESERVE

. . . in as spontaneous and nonstuttering a manner as possible. A potential client asks you what you charge. Just for argument's sake, let's compare two approaches. "My standard rate is $130 an hour, but I may adjust that up or down depending on your specific needs" certainly sounds a lot better than "Oh, yes, my rate. Of course. Well, it depends, you know, on the job. . . . But in this case, I guess, um, maybe, I don't know, $130 an hour?"

Which person would you want to hand over your money to? The crystal-clear communicator or the muddled, gun-shy mush-mouth? Practice with a friend; practice in front of a mirror. Whatever it takes—just make sure when you're asked about what you charge, your answer matches the level of professionalism you want to convey.

For your own clarity, you also need to know what your range of rates is: hourly, projectwise, weekly. Being clear about them ahead of time helps you to be clear with potential clients in the moment.

Note: the two main steps here—getting clear on what you want to make and practicing asking for it—can also be employed when looking for a new salaried job or if you are seeking a raise at one of your current permalancing gigs.

LEARN TO BID

In many businesses, a client approaches several vendors to take on a particular project. In a case such as this, you will often be asked to bid on the job. This means that others are bidding, too. The temptation in a situation like this is to bid as low as possible, in hopes that the person hiring is concerned with nothing more than the bottom line and you'll win the job. This is a dangerous approach and will usually come back to bite you in that fleshy region at the southern end of your spine. First, you stand the chance of underbidding so much that you look like you don't have a true grasp of what rates are in your business, therefore making you look unprofessional and uninformed about your own industry. Second, you should never bank on price alone to get you a job. You want to highlight the fact that you have the right talent, skills, and acumen to get the job done better than anyone else bidding, not just look like the cheapest one on the list. Third, if you are dealing with a client whose only concern is getting someone cheaply, they will eventually find someone even cheaper than you. And finally, if you routinely bid way too low, not only are you biting the hand that feeds you—which is, of course, *your* hand—but word will get out that you charge these ridiculously low rates, and trying to increase your income once you've established that kind of cheapo rep is going to be rather tricky.

RUN A TIGHT SHIP

You are a business. Do not forget that. And how you run your business is as important as how you do your work. This can be tricky for some freelancers, who, in most cases, want to spend their time doing what they love. "I was an art major, not a business major!" you cry in your defense. Well, big shocker—if you want to have your own business you need to know how to . . . you know . . . run your own business. Unless you can hire someone else to do so—and that is certainly a sensible and viable option—you have got to buck up and take care of things yourself.

BUILD YOUR SKILL SET

You should always be seeking to raise the standards for the quality of work that you do. This may mean taking a class or two, developing a new skill, or seeking evaluation from a top dog in your particular field. If you want to remain competitive, you have to stay sharp. If you're computer-phobic, but the growing trend in your field is to use a particular designing software, for example, you need to learn how to use that software, even if your preference is to go the analog route. You need that skill in your toolbox in case someone asks for it, or you risk looking hopelessly behind the times.

STAY ON TOP OF YOUR INDUSTRY

A key part of staying on top of your game is to be constantly evaluating trends and advances in your field of work. If you offer a product, look at what kinds of new developments are on the market. If you offer a service, be constantly looking at others who offer that service, and see how they present themselves and their work. Learn from what they appear to be doing right—and wrong.

STAY ORGANIZED

When Joe first went freelance, he found himself griping to an acquaintance about how invoices that he had sent to clients often went missing or unpaid for weeks or sometimes months at a time. His friend, Edgar, a grizzled old freelance photographer, pulled him aside and coached him.

"You've got no follow-through," the older man said. "The job doesn't end when you finish the work. Making sure they get the invoice is part of your job, too!"

For such a crusty gent, Edgar had nailed down a remarkably polite way of making sure he got paid. Each time he mailed out an invoice, he called the client several days afterward and asked three questions:

- "Did you receive my invoice?"
- "Is it in proper form?"
- "How long does it usually take your office to issue payment?"

Three simple questions was all it took to (a) impress upon the client that Edgar was serious about getting paid, (b) indicate that he expected to be treated professionally by the client, and (c) extract a subtle promise of payment by a certain date. If he didn't receive the check by the promised date, the client got a phone call.

If you want to be considered a professional, you must run your business affairs professionally. This means establishing fixed office-management habits that ensure consistent actions every time. Here's what we're talking about.

- **KNOW THE RULES OF THE PAYMENT GAME.** Every industry has its own expectations of payment. A cranky plumber friend of ours—a self-employed tradesman—once complained that a customer had him wait five weeks for payment on a job. We were stunned, but not for the reason you'd think. In our business, four to six weeks is a customary delay. But most plumbers expect payment at point of service. Every field of work has different expectations. Know what they are, play by the rules, and hold your clients to them, too.

- **EXECUTE PAPERWORK QUICKLY.** Whether it's a contract, an invoice, or some other document, your life will be made much simpler if you get it off your desk as quickly as possible. If this is a challenge for you or you hate interrupting your work flow to deal with business, budget one morning or afternoon a week to take care of all paperwork.

- **FOLLOW UP PROPERLY.** If you meet a potential client on June 1 to talk about a possible venture, don't wait until July 1 to follow up. The modern business world expects follow-ups to occur within one week's time, unless otherwise stated. Similarly, if you meet with a customer or client and make any sort of promise, get back to them when you said you would. That's how you would expect to be treated. *Write down every commitment you make.* If for some reason you can't make good on your promise, follow up anyway and tell them why. Even if *they* don't make good on their promises to *you*, you can train them over time to meet your expectations. Know what you stand for, and stick to it.

- **RETURN CALLS PROMPTLY.** How many times has someone explained away a long delay in response with that lame excuse "I've been swamped"? Expunge this phrase from your lexicon. It's horse hockey. Newsflash: it's the twenty-first century, and we're all swamped. If someone leaves a voice mail message for you, log it in and get back to them within twenty-four hours. E-mail etiquette is slightly different, we know, but even here you should set a high standard for yourself, such as committing to get back to an e-mail correspondent within one to three days. If you need to, set aside one hour a day to return calls and e-mails.

- **NEVER BE LATE, NEVER BE LATE, NEVER BE LATE.** The world does not owe you a living. Your client has made a choice to hire you. If you do a great job but are consistently late, they can easily choose someone else the next time around. We are, frankly, stunned at how many freelancers have a problem sticking to deadlines. The etiquette here is clear: you must call the client *as soon as* you know or suspect you will not deliver on time.

TIME TO HANG IT UP?

We happen to think the life of an independent worker is richly rewarding. But we realize that it's not for everyone—and so should you. Assuming you have not been thrust into this position involuntarily by a layoff, assuming you once envisioned working independently as highly desirable, it's entirely possible that you are still not cut out to work for yourself. The reasons are various: You may not like the solitary life. You may not like the social life, either, or the schmoozing necessary to network with and win clients in your particular field. You may not like the hustle. You may not like the hours. Learn to listen to these important emotional and psychological signals. And then listen to your finances as well.

- If you are repeatedly raiding an old 401(k) . . .
- If you consistently cannot earn what you need to cover your average monthly expenses . . .
- If you rely more on credit cards than real cash to pay your way . . .
- If you have been without health insurance for years because you simply cannot afford it . . .

then it might be time to hang it up. Get the résumés out, start scanning online job postings, and tell everyone you know that you're looking for a full-time gig. If you still harbor a longing to freelance, consider taking a part-time gig *in the same line of work* as a way of generating some steady income while still working on your own projects and dreams.

PRACTICE PROSPERITY CONSCIOUSNESS

Sometimes it's hard to stay positive and open about your income and the people who provide you with it. It makes sense to folks that negative people get lackluster results. Still, it is sometimes more difficult to convince people that upbeat, positive folks get better results. But it's true: staying upbeat no matter your current circumstances can pull you through tough times. Stay focused on the successes you *have* had, the clients you *have* snared, the progress you *have* made, and more of the same will come your way. You will also feel a lot better.

LEARN TO SAY YES

The wife of a screenwriter friend once discarded an old alligator-skin handbag that was beyond repair. Before it could be whisked away by the sanitation department, Walter dug it out of the trash and stripped off all the leather. He brought the mishmash of pieces to a shoemaker in the city where they lived and presented the guy with a challenge: "Can you make me a wallet out of these pieces?"

The shoemaker did a double take. "I repair shoes," he said. "I don't know anything about wallets."

Walter is persistent, a good trait for a screenwriter. Instead of walking away, he persuaded the man, using every bit of logic he could dream up. "Of *course* you can do it," he said. "You work with leather every day. You know how it behaves. You're the only one in town with the equipment capable of stitching through it. You're the man for the job."

"I've never done it before," the man protested.

"I drew a sketch," Walter countered. "All you have to do is cut the pieces to size, lay them on top of each other, and stitch it."

"I suppose," said the shoemaker. "But I wouldn't even know how to charge you."

"Charge me whatever it takes you to repair a pair of shoes. If you spend more time than that, charge me as if you did two pairs of shoes."

The upshot: two days later, Walter had a perfectly good wallet for little more than twenty dollars. And the shoemaker had added a new skill to his repertoire and earned some confidence. The lesson? Think carefully before turning down work that seems outside your experience. Very often, the outside world doesn't pigeonhole us as much as we pigeonhole ourselves.

An artist who pushes himself just a little bit can embark on a new side career building Web sites. A fitness coach can move beyond weights to Pilates and yoga. And on and on. If you're asked to do something that you have never done before but that employs skills you already have, don't be too quick to turn it down. If you don't have the skills but are intrigued, take a class and bone up.

LEARN TO SAY NO

On the other hand, saying no to a job can help you to hone your instincts about which jobs are a good fit and which are better left to other suckers. The tendency for the gig-to-gig worker is to scream "yes!" to virtually any offer of work, because of the fear that it could be the last offer for a long time. However, not all clients are desirable. You have to believe that more work is out there and coming to you as long as you stay committed. You also want to avoid clients who will underpay and overdemand. Unless you are absolutely strapped for cash, saying no every once in a while is a good thing to do.

A couple years ago, we were approached by a publisher to work on a rather substantial book. When they asked us for our price, we gave them our standard rate: not too high, because it wasn't going to be that difficult, and not too low, because it was going to take a fair amount of time. The response we got back was "Sorry, that's way beyond what we're willing to pay. We just can't pay that." Instead of saying, "Oh—well, we can do it for half that price," we simply said, "Thanks so much for considering us. Perhaps we can work together in the future. Best of luck with the book." And we promptly forgot about them and never expected to hear from them any time soon.

Flash forward about six weeks. . . .

We got a call from the very same publisher. They had hired

someone who was willing to take the much lower rate. And guess what? That person did not have the experience or expertise to get the job done right. The publisher had let that person go and was now in a bind because the project was behind schedule. They hired us to do the job at our original asking price—which was almost double what they had said their maximum payment would be. Saying no got us what we wanted and gave us a big confidence boost.

ENLIST OTHERS IN THE FIGHT

OK. So maybe you're not a joiner. Every time we say to seek the advice, input, or camaraderie of others in your field, you tense up and crawl back in your work cave. As we've said before, get over it. Being in business for yourself means consistently pushing your own limits. It can also be very isolating work. Meeting others who face the same struggles, who have the same issues with clients, who continue to stress over bidding for jobs can provide you with the kind of perspective that can reinvigorate you. You may get answers from these folks, or you may not. You may just get a sympathetic ear (which many freelancers rarely get from their office-bound friends, who don't really understand what it is we do). No matter the result, connecting with people in your situation—as long as it doesn't turn into some kind of mopefest—can help you stay positive about your career and earning potential. If you feel like your fortitude is waning and you need a good ol' kick in the can to stay the course, consider making a "bet" with yourself. Sites like stickK (stickk.com) can help you stay committed, simply by making failure such an unappealing option. (In some cases, people who use stickK to reach goals commit to donating money to a group they absolutely despise should they fail as a means of forcing them to follow through on their commitments, whether it be staying with a savings regimen, seeking a certain number of new clients, or losing weight.) Whatever your means of motivation, find it.

In short, be aware, be dedicated, and be constantly reassessing. From this moment forward, cultivate a new, positive outlook. Working independently is not just something you *want* to do; it's something you *are* doing. You're doing it right now. Stop behaving and speaking to yourself as if you *want* to be an independent worker someday. You are one already. Own it. Love it. Broadcast it. Staying positive and focused will carry you through.

WHAT TO DO

Being prosperous doesn't just mean staying focused on your income. It also means doing everything that you can to keep your business on track and running smoothly. Here are some exercises that can help you.

- List everyone who paid you last year. Assess your income providers. Where does most of your money come from? Is the majority of your money coming from a limited number of clients or outlets?
- Make a list of five new ways you would like to see your business grow. This could include a list of new clients you would like to approach or current clients whose business you would like to increase. It could be customers or outlets you want to attract or something more tangible like new office space. For each of these five items, do the following:

  - Brainstorm steps you could take to make each happen.
  - List any roadblocks that you feel are preventing you from making them happen. Make a plan for how you could overcome them.
  - If necessary, think about new Dream Accounts that you would need to help move things along.
  - Do a little detective work. What is the going rate for your kind of service or product in your area, or the area where you do the most work? Are you charging too little? Too much?

- Optional touchy-feely exercise for this chapter: Write out a vivid description of what you want your business to look like in one, five, and ten years. Do you have employees? Are you in a different location? Who are your customers? How much do you make? Be as detailed and descriptive as possible. If you can't see it, you won't achieve it.

CHAPTER 12

THE FINAL WORD ON FINANCIAL EMPOWERMENT

One of the most colorful, renowned, and prosperous independent workers who ever lived has his mug plastered on the hundred-dollar bill. That's right—Benjamin Franklin, one of our fave founders, had a life that exemplified everything we hold dear about being an entrepreneur: hard work, limitless creativity, and a fantastic savings regimen. Here's a guy who started out life indentured to his brother, without two pence to rub together, and who went on to become the media mogul of his day.

Franklin's vision for the future of the colonies featured a country full of self-sufficient entrepreneurs: farmers, artisans, blacksmiths, bakers, and so on, all self-employed, running their own outfits. His story exemplified that. After setting out on his own and starting a printing business that eventually included newspapers, books, and his famed *Poor Richard's Almanack,* Franklin raked in so much cash that he was able to retire at the age of forty-two, after which he devoted himself to philanthropy, statesmanship, and every once in a while, the lovely ladies.

His fortune tripled during the Revolutionary War, while founders like Thomas Jefferson and others struggled to make ends meet. But it wasn't all luck of the draw. "Poor Richard" was hardly poor—but he was also a thrifty little saver.

If you rocket forward to the present day, isn't America moving ever closer to being the country of self-sufficient businessfolk that Franklin originally imagined it should be?

Think about it: the number of independent workers is already on the upswing. Compound that with the fact that every time people are laid off, not all of them return to the workplace. Many decide to strike out on their own and run their own businesses. With every corporate shakedown, every time benefits are cut back, every time another pension goes the way of the dodo, we are moving closer and closer to the vision old Ben had of America nearly 250 years ago.

So remember: you are a part of a grand dream born of revolution and embodied by one of the most notable gents—and savers—in history.

OUR KIND OF BENEFITS

We have spent the bulk of this book dealing with the financial challenges that freelancers face. But truth be told, we all have a lot of fantastic things going on as well.

So we would like to close things out by celebrating our spirit and independence.

We think it's quite telling that every time we get a little down, a bit frustrated, and we dare ask ourselves, *Should we stick with this?* the answer always comes back, *Absolutely*. We are convinced it is due in no small part to the kind of money-management advice we have presented in this book. This, combined with a commitment to run our business like any proper company would (minus the dress code), has made it possible for us to keep pursuing our dreams. In short, our ability to manage our finances continues to give us the opportunity to do what we love.

Independent workers need to pay closer attention to the financial ins and outs of their lives than many regular salaried people do. Most freelancers know a lot more about taxes than salaried counterparts who merely have to check a withholding box when they start their job and sign their tax forms come April. Shopping for health care is another adventure, as is maneuvering various investment vehicles and options. But none of this is a bad thing. Skills like these can help you—whether or not you're still self-employed—weather the tough times. They give you the ability to create a viable plan for the good and bad stretches in your life. Adaptability and flexibility are the hallmarks of the successful independent entrepreneur, and they serve any human being well.

We've also enjoyed seeing how the management and finance skills that we have developed as freelancers have seeped into every fiber of our existence. This book is about organizing your money. And being organized is never a bad thing. Ask any work-at-home mom who has to juggle the house, her kids' schedules, and her own life whether she relies on organizational skills. You betcha.

Kate, the hairstylist, has already noticed results beyond money since she got serious about her finances. "When it comes to paying bills and running the house, I think that I'm much more thorough in all of it because I've had to become so organized in my own personal business in order to make it work," she explains.

So whether you find yourself working independently by choice or because of circumstances currently beyond your control, there are lessons here that you can carry with you into your day-to-day activities, at work and beyond.

Working for yourself may be harder than working at a conventional job, but the rewards are greater. Below we've listed some of the things that the people we interviewed said that they appreciated about the path they have chosen.

THINGS INDEPENDENT WORKERS ARE GRATEFUL FOR

"I enjoy being creative and making my own work."

"I love being able to do something I care about, not just what my boss cares about."

"I like being able to take a three-day weekend whenever I want."

"I feel more in control of my finances."

"Fewer meetings! I don't miss office meetings that go nowhere."

"Being able to rent and decorate the office of my dreams was such a thrill."

"I feel like an adult for the first time in my life."

"I love owning my own business and making my own hours. I feel proud about that."

"I make my own decisions and set my own schedule."

So how about you? Is there something that you're grateful for, something that keeps you going even when the bills stack up and the checks are late? Take out a piece of paper right now and write down ten things you like about your work life. Do it. We'll wait.

Tick, tock, tick, tock . . .

Done? Now look at that list. Not bad, is it? This joy that you can summon, this vim and vigor that infuse your bones when you think about the ass-kicking aspects of your life, should be carried over into your every day. Hang on to them, relish them, run them up the flagpole and salute them. The sense of accomplishment and satisfaction embodied by what you just wrote on that sheet of paper will trickle down (not in a Reagan kind of way, but in a feed-your-monkey kind of way) and drastically affect the way you feel about yourself. As the crooners preached, you've got to ac-cent-tchu-ate the positive and eliminate the negative. After just a few months of working diligently with this system, you will find comfort and so much more in knowing that you have a plan.

IMAGE IS EVERYTHING

Before this book, you may have looked at your whole picture and felt a little lopsided. You loved what you did, but you had nagging doubts and insecurities because the financial side of your life was simply not as rewarding as the work that you were doing on a daily basis. But now that you're working to get to a place where you are saving money, where you can see concrete goals ahead of you and know that you're constantly moving toward them, you will start to feel joyful about your life as a whole.

The effect that money issues can have on well-being is well documented. In 2006, a survey conducted by the American Psychological Association found that money is the top source of stress for adults. It is certainly the top stressor for freelancers. But once you get your money under control, you can relax and enjoy your life and your work more. This is exactly what Kate, the hairstylist, discovered: "Now that my finances are in better shape, being an independent businessperson hasn't been all that difficult." When we asked if she'd ever want to take a full-time job, she made a noise like a cat coughing up a fur ball. "Ugh!" she said. "I get a physical reaction just thinking about it. I wouldn't. Absolutely not. I couldn't imagine having someone dictate when I can take days off or go on vacation. It would feel insulting to my own sense of organization and my own person."

Well said, Kate!

You will have the same feeling, too, if you don't already. You will no longer have that lopsided, insecure, vulnerable feeling that so many people have when they work for The Man. You'll feel confident as you move ahead toward your goals, because it feels good to have a plan for financial success.

And now, we'll let you in on a dirty little secret: everyone on the planet is working for themselves; they just don't know it. The guy in the cubicle thinks he is working for the boss and a faceless corporation, but he's dead wrong. He's working for himself, his family, his future. The sooner you let that sink in and start treating your money as the lifeblood of your existence, something to be respected, something you alone earn for yourself, the better off you will be.

For many of us, it's important to revamp the image we have of the members of our independent working community. Too often we view ourselves as fly-by-the-seat-of-our-pantsers, people just barely keeping it together. We are not. We are self-sufficient businesspeople. Self-starters. Entrepreneurs. People with serious gumption and chutzpah.

This takes on importance for couples, too. If you're part of a couple, you *must* talk about finances as part of your relationship image. And you had better come to an agreement about your goals, too. If you are in, or considering, a long-term partnership, stop talking about the sex and love and all the rest of that gooey crap and get your financial cards on the table. The nookie will still be there. In fact, it may even be hotter. The number one thing that splits up a couple? Infidelity. Number two? Finances. Don't dangerously mix both of those naughty practices by indulging in financial infidelity, either: saying one thing to your partner, then doing the opposite when you're off on your own with the credit card in your hot little hands. Get brutally honest with each other about your fiscal responsibilities. This will also give you the kind of support you need to stick with your new savings and money-management regimen.

If you're not in a relationship, consider joining forces with others and forming a financial support group. We've said it before, and we'll say it again: get involved with the freelance community. Check out the sites we recommend in the appendix. Log on, tune in, and rev up your mood. You'll learn things; you'll gain perspective. You can also feel free to get together the old-fashioned, Luddite way: meet together in person on a regular basis. Have a potluck. Have some drinks and free appetizers at a happy hour and plot your mission to take over the world. Having a support system can help to dispel the clouds and yank you out of your financial doldrums. Above all, be accountable to someone.

So stick to the plan, sure. But also take time to celebrate what it is you like about your work life. Revel in the unlimited potential your situation presents. Embrace the skills and techniques you are developing that will only make you more efficient in all areas of your life. Remind yourself that you are a competent businessperson working for yourself and those you love. Stay on track, share your frustrations and triumphs with others, and keep on keeping on. Soon, you and your monkey will walk off into the sunset, cash in your pockets, opposable thumbs entwined.

Before you know it, you'll be saying to yourself, "Well, damn. . . . Maybe I *can* pull this off."

You can. You will.

APPENDIX

The following is a beginner's guide to exploring the world of personal finance for freelancers. To keep this list brief, we have focused primarily on items mentioned or promised in the course of the book. To these resources, we would humbly add our own. We welcome visitors and e-mails via our Web site, feed-the-monkey.com.

Personal Financial Software

Web- and Software-Based

Quicken (quicken.intuit.com)

Quick Books (quickbooks.intuit.com)

Web-Based Only

Mint.com (mint.com)

Geezeo (geezeo.com)

Yodlee (yodlee.com)

Wesabe (wesabe.com)

Buxfer (buxfer.com)

Money Strands (money.strands.com)

Mvelopes (mvelopes.com)

Personal-Finance Blogs

GetRichSlowly (getrichslowly.org)

The Simple Dollar (thesimpledollar.com)

I Will Teach You to Be Rich (iwillteachyoutoberich.com)

Freelance and Productivity Blogs

Freelance Switch (freelanceswitch.com)

Freelance Folder (freelancefolder.com)

Mrs. Micah: Finance for a Freelance Life (mrsmicah.com)

Guerilla Freelancing (guerillafreelancing.com)

43 Folders (43folders.com)

Web Sites That Write Frequently on the Topic of Personal Finance

CNN Money (money.cnn.com)

Yahoo Finance (finance.yahoo.com/personal-finance)

MSNBC (msnbc.msn.com)

CNBC (cnbc.com)

The Motley Fool (fool.com)

The Wallet (blogs.wsj.com/wallet/)

Planet Money (http://www.npr.org/blogs/money/)

Personal-Finance Magazines

Money

SmartMoney

Kiplinger's Personal Finance

Credit Counseling Services

Choose a nonprofit consumer credit counseling service affiliated with either of the following:

National Foundation for Credit Counseling (nfcc.org)

Association of Independent Consumer Credit Counseling Agencies (aiccca.org)

Online Calculators

Hugh's Mortgage and Financial Calculators (hughchou.org/calc)

Dinkytown (dinkytown.net)

Bankrate (bankrate.com)

Mortgage-calc (mortgage-calc.com)

CNN Money.com (cgi.money.cnn.com/tools/)

Online Banks

Discover Bank (discoverbank.com)

EmigrantDirect (emigrantdirect.com)

E*TRADE Bank (us.etrade.com/e/t/banking)

HSBC (us.hsbc.com)

iGObanking (igobanking.com)

ING Direct (ingdirect.com)

MyBankingDirect (mybankingdirect.com)

State Farm Bank (statefarm.com)

UmbrellaBank (umbrellabank.com)

VirtualBank (virtualbank.com)

Investment Firms

The following are reputable firms that offer small-business retirement plans—including individual 401(k)s.

VANGUARD (vanguard.com)

(877) 662–7447

Minimums: account minimums vary. Most require $3,000 to open retirement and nonretirement accounts. Once minimums are met, you can contribute as little as $100 via monthly automatic deposit.

See https://personal.vanguard.com/us/accounttypes/smallbusiness.

T. ROWE PRICE (individual.troweprice.com)

(800) 638–5660

Minimums: $2,500 for nonretirement; $1,000 for all retirement accounts. Minimums are waived for both types with a $50 monthly automatic deposit.

See http://individual.troweprice.com/public/Retail/Retirement/Small-Business-Retirement-Plans.

FIDELITY INVESTMENTS (fidelity.com)

(800) fiDELITY

Minimums: $2,500 for nonretirement and retirement accounts. The minimum is waived for retirement accounts with a $200 monthly automatic deposit.

See http://personal.fidelity.com/products/retirement/getstart/newacc/keogh.shtml.cvsr.

SCHWAB (schwab.com)

(866) 232–9890

Minimums: $1,000 for nonretirement, IRA, and Roth IRA accounts; no minimums for business retirement accounts (simple IRA, SEP-IRA, and individual 401(k)); all minimums waived with $100 monthly automatic deposit.

See http://www.schwab.com/public/schwab/home/account_types/small_business_retirement?cmsid=P-987153&lvl1=home&lvl2=account_types&.

Reading List

Getting Things Done: The Art of Stress-Free Productivity, by David Allen (Penguin, 2002).

Just Give Me the Answer$: Expert Advisors Address Your Most Pressing Financial Questions, by Sheryl Garrett, with Marie Swift and the Garrett Planning Network (Kaplan Business Books, 2004).

The Complete Tightwad Gazette, by Amy Dacyczyn (Villard Books, 1998).

The Millionaire Next Door, by Thomas J. Stanley and William D. Danko (Pocket Books, 1998).

The Richest Man in Babylon, by George S. Clason (several editions available).

Think and Grow Rich, by Napoleon Hill (several editions available).

Independent Worker News and Advocacy

Freelancers Union (freelancersunion.org)

Freelancers Union blog (freelancersunion.org/blog)

National Association for the Self-Employed (nase.org)

Health Insurance

eHealthInsurance (eHealthInsurance.com)

Freelancers Union (freelancersunion.org)

National Association for the Self-Employed (nase.org)

Check your trade association to find out if you are eligible for a group rate.

Fee-Paid Financial Planners

Garrett Planning Network (garrettplanningnetwork.com)

National Association of Personal Financial Advisors (napfa.org)

Other Web Sites Worth Investigating

StickK (stickk.com)

SmartyPig (smartypig.com)

IRS Resources

Internal Revenue Service (irs.gov)

IRC 183 (Profit Motive) (irs.gov/businesses/small/article/0,,id=208400,00.html)

529 Plans

Saving for College (savingforcollege.com)

ACKNOWLEDGMENTS

We are grateful to have received the kind assistance of so many talented individuals, traditionally employed and self-employed alike. For helping us get our message into print, we must thank Lindsay Orman and Jo Rodgers, our editors at Three Rivers Press. We bow deeply before copy editor Hilary Roberts, who sharpened our prose; designers Kyle Kolker, Gretchen Achilles, and Laura Palese, who made the book look spiffy; and production editor Mark Birkey, who guided the book through the whole process. We must also add a special note of thanks to the rest of the publishing and marketing team at Three Rivers: Philip Patrick, Heather Proulx, Jay Sones, and Samantha Choy.

We are indebted to our agent, Yfat Reiss Gendell, who nurtured this concept on its way to the big city. We are equally grateful for the encouragement of Yfat's cohort, Peter Harrison McGuigan, and their crackerjack team at Foundry Literary + Media, notably Kendra Jenkins and Hannah Brown Gordon.

We owe a debt, too, to those who graciously submitted to our interviews during the research process: J. D. Roth of Get Rich Slowly (getrichslowly.org), Hugh Chou (hughchou.com), and tax demystifier Stewart Minikes. We also thank the financial planners of the Garrett Planning Network: Jeff Kostis of JK Financial Planning (jkfinancialplanning.com), Kathleen Campbell of Campbell financial Partners (campbellfp.com), and Sherrill St. Germain of New Means Financial Planning (newmeans.com). Many thanks to you all, ladies and gentlemen, and long may your businesses prosper.

Lastly, we could not have written this book without the input of colleagues, friends, and family members. Because no one likes getting financially naked before the world, we promised these individuals we would respect their privacy. And so you know them as Dave, Erin, James, Kate, Karl, Sid, Carol, Emily, Sarah, Edgar, Walter, Grouchy Plumber Guy, and a few others who go wholly unnamed.

Though we consulted all these folks—experts and freelancers in the trenches alike—any factual errors or misstatements are purely our own.

We thank you all from the bottoms of our hearts.

INDEX

ABOUT THE AUTHORS

Denise is a writer and producer who loves traveling. Joe is a writer and producer who loves being dragged wherever Denise wants to go. They have written a number of books both for adults and for children, on their own and together as a husband-and-wife team. Their reporting has appeared in nationally known newspapers and magazines. They live in North Carolina.